A Bibliography of The Village Press

1903·1938

A BIBLIOGRAPHY OF
The Village Press

BY MELBERT B. CARY, JR.

◆

INCLUDING AN ACCOUNT OF THE
GENESIS OF THE PRESS BY FREDERIC W. GOUDY
AND A PORTION OF THE 1903 DIARY OF
WILL RANSOM, CO-FOUNDER

OAK KNOLL BOOKS
EDWARD RIPLEY-DUGGAN
NICHOLAS T. SMITH, PUBLISHER

New Castle, Delaware

Originally published in 1938 by The
Press of the Woolly Whale, New York City

Republished in 1981 with the permission of
Yale University. This edition is reproduced
from an original in the Yale University Library.

The Publishers would like to express their
appreciation to Donald B. Engley, Associate
University Librarian, Yale University, for his
cooperation in making this project possible.

Copyright © 1938, 1956 by Melbert B. Cary, Jr.

Library of Congress Catalogue Card Number: 81-52218

International Standard Book Numbers:

Oak Knoll Books: 0-938768-05-0
Edward Ripley-Duggan: 0-9606532-0-1
Nicholas T. Smith: 0-935164-08-1

Printed in the United States of America

Order from:

Oak Knoll Books
414 Delaware Street
New Castle, Delaware 19720

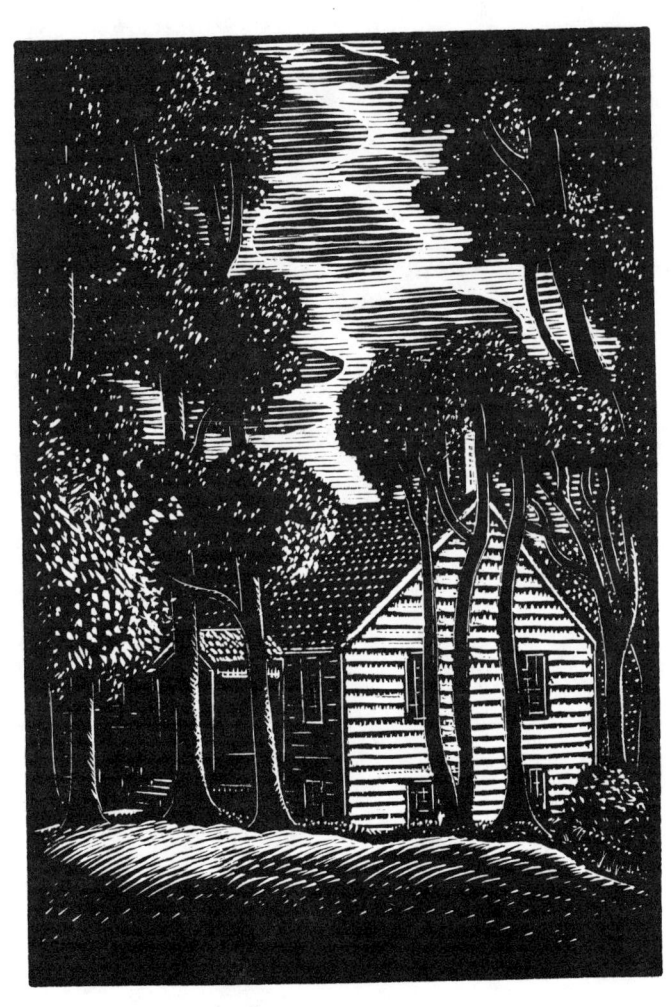

THE OLD MILL, MARLBOROUGH, NEW YORK
(WOODCUT BY CHARLES W. SMITH)

1903 · 1938

A BIBLIOGRAPHY OF
The Village Press

BY MELBERT B. CARY, JR.

◆

INCLUDING AN ACCOUNT OF THE
GENESIS OF THE PRESS BY FREDERIC W. GOUDY
AND A PORTION OF THE 1903 DIARY OF
WILL RANSOM, CO-FOUNDER

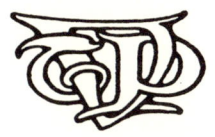

MCMXXXVIII
The Press of the Woolly Whale
New York, N.Y.

COPYRIGHT 1938 BY MELBERT B. CARY, JR.
Printed in the U. S. A.

Contents

THE VILLAGE PRESS, AN INTRODUCTION   1
    by Frederic W. Goudy

THE FIRST DAYS OF THE VILLAGE PRESS   33
    from the Diary of Will Ransom

A BIBLIOGRAPHY OF THE VILLAGE PRESS   45
    by Melbert B. Cary, Jr.

PUBLICATIONS OF THE PRESS

PARK RIDGE, ILLINOIS	1903-1904	51
HINGHAM, MASSACHUSETTS	1904-1906	61
NEW YORK CITY, NEW YORK	1906-1913	75
FOREST HILLS GARDENS, N.Y.	1913-1923	117
MARLBOROUGH, NEW YORK	from 1923	153
INDEX		193

FREDERIC W. GOUDY, 1936

1903  1938

THE VILLAGE PRESS

An Introduction

BY FREDERIC W. GOUDY

THE VILLAGE PRESS had its real beginnings almost a decade before the Press itself actually was set up; and I do not wish to claim for it at this late date any of the master motives so often and so easily found to glorify or add a glamour of romance to a simple prosaic venture entirely lacking romantic environment; a venture which, as a matter of fact, came about so casually as almost to be hardly worth noting.

That the Press has persisted for nearly two score years, that it represents a distinct and consistent attempt by its proprietors toward an ideal of craft and craftsmanship, though falling far short of the ideal aimed at, may, I hope, furnish sufficient reasons to justify my belief that the story of the steps leading to its founding will prove of interest.

The Village Press: An Introduction

Most private presses have been established for some specific reason—(a) the dissemination of propaganda, religious, political or other; (b) a form of dilettantism, as when one with leisure, literary taste, and sufficient means to gratify personal pleasures may develop a mere whim into a pleasant occupation; (c) a press to preserve in interesting form some special literature, or for the purpose of furnishing worthwhile matter as examples of fine printing; (d) or it may be a press established with the thought of commercial gain as the principal aim; that is, expecting to receive a financial return commensurate with the degree of fine workmanship and craft presented in its publications.

In which category The Village Press belongs may be inferred from the story itself.

In 1895 in Chicago I was a bookkeeper, a self-taught accountant of sorts, in a book shop which dealt almost exclusively in second-hand school books. I can't say truthfully that this connection was more than a mere job, or that it contributed in any way to bookish feeling or inclination toward fine printing. I already was an omniverous reader, since as a boy I had access to my father's rather good library. He was a teacher, a superintendent of schools and a reader himself, a fact which probably accounts for my own predilection for such books as *The Vicar of Wakefield, Vathek, Undine, Picciola, Piers Ploughman* and many books which few youths of the present generation know even by name.

My connection, however, as bookkeeper there did bring me into closer contact in a business way with dealers in books not entirely for school use. My immediate "boss" was James D. Farquhar, the manager of the store. He gave up his position there not long after I had "quit" and established himself in a similar business. For several years I kept up a desultory friendly contact with him, but finally lost sight of him. This spring (1937) while on a short trip to Los Angeles I was pleased to receive a telephone call from him, he having seen a newspaper item regarding my visit there. He called at my hotel and we reminisced for an hour or so over our relations together more than forty years before. He remembered that even in those days I showed a leaning toward design and better printing, and he was kind enough to say that, due to my preaching about such things, I had opened his mind to a greater and lasting appreciation of books and bookmaking. Probably the bits of information I picked up

The Village Press: An Introduction

on my frequent noonday visits to the bookstore of A. C. McClurg & Co., then at the corner of Wabash Avenue and Madison Street, and which I retailed to him, are what he remembers.

It was on these visits to McClurg's that my attention was first drawn to books which were definite examples of typographic art and craft. Until then it had not occurred to me that the physical appearance of one book might present some pleasing quality not found in another, although I do recall very clearly that almost from the time when I could read understandingly, I sensed unconsciously that certain books, apart from their subject matter, seemed to invite reading more than others, but as yet I was not sufficiently interested to wonder why this might be so.

With no definite thought of ever becoming a book-collector, my acute yearning for information led me to make occasional purchases, as my meager financial status permitted, of books and magazines on printing or of examples of printing, to satisfy a curiosity on these points which in some way had been aroused. I took to haunting the Saints' and Sinners' Corner in McClurg's—the corner hallowed by such men as Dr. Frank Gunsaulus, Francis Wilson, Frank Morris, Dr.

The Village Press: An Introduction

Stryker, Eugene Field, W. Irving Way and other well-known bibliophiles. Mr. George Millard, in charge of the rare books, was the guiding spirit, the patron saint, of the corner. I feel even now the thrill that came to me on one of my noon-hour visits there when I saw Mr. Millard talking to a man whom I at once recognized as the great actor—of his day and style—Sol Smith Russell, who also was a great book lover and collector. Of course, a poor, unknown bookkeeper like me wouldn't know any of these distinguished collectors, but later I am proud to have come to know and to talk with many of them as a fellow book lover (sometimes of books not yet mine, but of which by use of library and the book magazines I already knew well).

Mr. Millard, jovial, kindly soul that he was, noted my frequent visits, all without profit to his department, but who nevertheless never failed to reply cheerfully and fully to any inquiry regarding his treasures.

I have told elsewhere how the sight of a Vale Press copy of the *Poems of Sir John Suckling* first stirred my imagination regarding its type, the hand-made paper and its general get-up as a private press publication. At that time this particular book, to me, was an aris-

The Village Press: An Introduction

tocrat belonging to an aristocracy of craft and typographic art. A new leaf in the book of my life was turned and my interest in fine bookmaking was born; a wide prospect was disclosed and a world that lay beyond the horizon of my imagination invited exploration. Just as Caxton's presses are the literary glory of Henry VII's reign, this book represented typographic glory for me.

Two or three years ago, Miss Fanny Borden, Librarian of Vassar College Library, at a talk I gave before a group of Vassar College students, remembered that I mentioned this book as the earliest inspirer of my, as yet, unawakened taste and desire for greater knowledge of private press publications, and kindly presented me with a copy of the Poems; not, of course, the actual copy I saw at McClurg's, but one of the same issue, which I note now is dated 1896, thus fixing the beginnings, the vision, it may be, of The Village Press itself.

The Vale Press publications were, I learned, set in a type designed by Charles Ricketts, an English portrait artist who added decorative wood engraving to his work and who executed his own initials, borders and illustrations in wood for the books he planned

The Village Press: An Introduction

and published. His books were not printed by him nor even printed by hand, as were the books issued by William Morris whom in point of time he followed. I can now see that Ricketts, in his own anxiety to avoid any suggestion of plagiarism of Morris's type, incorporated certain features in his font that he might not have included otherwise. It was entirely by chance that my attention was called to this particular book, and Mr. Millard, noting my evident interest in its appearance, brought to my attention books from Morris's Kelmscott Press which I had not as yet seen. He often showed me the latest importations of private press books and allowed me to share his enthusiasm for them. And then I began to frequent the Newberry Library, to read about books of an earlier vintage, buying books about books as I could spare their cost. Many of those bought then I have still in my own library.

This was several years after my first earlier visits to McClurg's. In the meantime I had left the second-hand school book office and had started a small commercial printing plant with the aid and co-operation of my friend Cyrus Lauron Hooper, a teacher I had met some years before. The Press was first called "The

The Village Press: An Introduction

Booklet Press," later renamed "The Camelot* Press." There came to us early in its existence the important (to us) job of printing *The Chap Book*, a bibelot just then brought to Chicago by two Harvard students, Stone & Kimball. I will speak of *The Chap Book* more particularly later in this paper.

The Press was doomed from the start for several reasons—first, because I hardly knew from practical experience which end of a metal type might be the printing end; second, lack of capital; and third the lack of business sense in the matter of charges for work performed. I imagine much of the work came to us because of the low price I put on it—that taste or arrangement were chargeable qualities was something more or less inexplicable to me; some say it is even yet true of me. Anyway, for the year or two that the Press survived, work of a desirable sort did trickle in and in sufficient amount to discourage the wolf at the door, not enough to drive him away, but at least enough to discourage him.

One of our earliest experiences—I say "our" but really it should be "my," as my friend Hooper was a

---

* Suggested by "Many-tower'd Camelot" in Tennyson's poem *The Lady of Shalott*.

The Village Press: An Introduction

Normal School principal and devoted no time to the Press—was a little announcement that my erstwhile friend, Robert Dillon, secretary of the Architectural Sketch Club, had me do every other week for the Club. He gave me the copy with no specifications other than "the announcement must be in the mail" at a certain time. I was free to exercise my own judgement as to size, shape and arrangement, *provided it didn't cost over two dollars*. As I think back, some of those cards must have required the work of a day or more; frequently they were in two or more colors, but I take pride in the fact that they never failed to go out on time. But I do recall with chagrin, as keen today as then, that owing to the fact that Dillon didn't wish to be bothered with "proof," on one of the announcements for him I spelled "chafing dish" with two f's; at least I passed the error, though my compositor (pressman, errand boy) may actually have set the matter.

It wasn't long after these announcements for the Club before there would now and then come a knock at the door and I would find a young woman there. "Is this the Camelot Press?" "Yes." "Was this (one of the Club announcements) done here?" "Yes." "Well, I am Secretary, Manager, something or other—of such and such Club. We'd like a little printing, etc., etc." When the Sheriff finally took over the details of closing the Press as a going concern, we were doing work that would be important even today. For one of our jobs I ordered from Boston the then new "Jenson" type which had been copied by the Dickinson Type Foundry (afterwards a branch of American Type Founders Co.) from William Morris's celebrated "Golden" type with which he began work at his Kelmscott Press. It was this type, an innovation then, in which I seemed to recognize qualities not present in other types easily available, but just what constituted the difference was as yet too subtle a matter for my limited knowledge. The type was 14 pt. size and I received a postal card acknowledgment of the order from the foundry with the added information that mine was the *first* order for it from Chicago.

It was at this time that I began to notice more particularly the productions of the private presses and began my study of them and especially of Morris's work. In the '90's, even now in some degree, the discipline of a living tradition was not generally part and parcel of American printers; it remained for Morris to revive and apply this tradition. The keen sense of rhythmic order and fine observance of restrained harmony shown in his printing reacted on my own innate feeling, and the influence of his motives in craft as represented by his printing is as strong today in my mind as then.

Among the last pieces of printing we did was a large four-page folder addressed to the subscribers to the Orchestral Association of which Theodore Thomas was the director. I forget for the moment which one of the officers of the Association called on me in person with the copy and plan, but I remember that the names signed to it represented actual millions in money, among them Marshall Field, Thomas Higginbotham, Lyman Gage, Charles Fay (who, I think, was the gentleman who saw me in my modest shop), as well as other well-known Chicago rich men.

I am recalling these bits of reminiscence as suggesting upon what foundation later The Village Press was erected. Before the Camelot Press finally closed, a friend of Mr. Hooper's, George Leland Hunter by name, then foreign re-write man on the Chicago *Tribune*, became a part of our organization because he was confident he could influence more customers to employ us. He and I didn't hit it off so well. Ignorant as I was of com-

The Village Press: An Introduction

mercial matters, he was even more ignorant of printing and it wasn't long after his advent he paid me a small amount and I retired from the Press; the Sheriff helped him to retire a few months later. I never saw him again but some years after I became a resident of New York City I found that he was the author of a sizable book on Oriental rugs—I hope he knew more about rugs than he knew about printing.

While operating the Camelot Press I found it at times difficult to get little bits of decorative material I thought might add to the appearance of the work in hand. Typefounders' ornaments in the years of the *fin de siècle* were as a rule stiff, often crude, and too trite for my taste. I had in my employ a young man named Bernard Nadal, of French descent. He got his job because he said he could set type—well, he could, but not much, if any, better than I, which, in fact, was no recommendation at all. But he did have some facility of design, and occasionally would supply a bit of decoration that I would use. I wouldn't buy the typefounders' ornaments and was unable to pay for professional designers' work, so his attempts helped out. And really it is due to him that I, later, became a decorative designer.

The Village Press: An Introduction

Someone has written that occasionally it is given to a young man to embark upon a joyous adventure, with tentative ideas as to goal, and yet presently to make an enduring mark. Ingalls Kimball, while a student at Harvard in the early '90's had developed a passion for the fashioning of good books, and with his classmate, Herbert Stone (son of Melville Stone), another enthusiast, he founded the publishing firm of Stone & Kimball; together they embarked upon just such an adventure from which flowed a lasting and far-flung unforseen influence.

It was while I was operating the Camelot Press that I came to know Herbert S. Stone and Ingalls Kimball. While still students at Harvard, they had begun the publishing of a slender fortnightly magazine called *The Chap Book*. The first volume was printed May, 1894, in Cambridge, Mass. It met with so much success that the publishers left Harvard, came to Chicago and through the introduction to them by my erstwhile friend and book-lover, the late W. Irving Way, I became the printer of the second volume. *The Chap Book* was an innovation in magazine format and contents. The publishers, no doubt, had been strongly influenced by the work of another young publishing

The Village Press: An Introduction

firm, Copeland & Day, who, in turn, were following closely the beginnings of what we now speak of as the revival of printing in England.

Mr. Ernest Elmo Calkins says that the magazine wrought in him a transformation; it was to me an inspiration as well as a transformation. In the offices of Stone & Kimball I met a number of writers and designers. As I was becoming more and more interested in design, I recall the thrill that was mine on being introduced to Tom Meteyard, the English artist, who had just designed for Stone & Kimball the cover for Stevenson's *The Ebb Tide,* and he showed me his drawing for it. He knew Stevenson personally, he said, and Richard Hovey, and Bliss Carman, and other well-known Boston literary celebrities. It was at this time I first met Hamlin Garland, a contributor to *The Chap Book. The Chap Book* brought to my notice the work of Aubrey Beardsley, William Sharp, Percival Pollard, T. B. Hapgood and others.

All these inconsequential contacts helped to broaden my field of study and strengthened my wish to know more of the work of those men whose names represented so much of idealism for me. Later, I did come to know more or less intimately such men as

The Village Press: An Introduction

Bruce Rogers, D.B. Updike, Bertram Grosvenor Goodhue, Bliss Carman, Alfred Pollard, Sir Emery Walker and many others.

After retiring from the Press, I returned to bookkeeping and occasionally tried my own hand at design. I had often watched Nadal work—he used a pencil and merely drew over the pencil lines in ink. I had a pencil too, and why not? My first attempts were sent to the *Inland Printer*. As they were not made on order I had no particular use for them and the *Inland*, I knew, often showed such designs in its pages. To my surprise the *Inland* actually printed them and gave me credit for their design and later, wonder of wonders! gave me an order to design a cover for the *Printer*. It is still extant (I hope not too much so). A sheet of ornaments I drew early in 1897 I sold to Marder, Luse & Co., typefounders in Chicago, and the sum they later paid me for a type design enabled me to pay railroad fare to take a position in Detroit as bookkeeper for the *Michigan Farmer*, an agricultural paper. While in Detroit I occasionally tried my hand at advertising designs for the Lawrence Publishing Company, who published the *Farmer*. I recall receiving an order from a St. Louis typefoundry for two sets of ornamental initials which I designed in pencil and Bertha (whom I had married in June '97) filled in the drawings in ink. Where they are now I do not know. In the late fall of 1899 I returned to Chicago and began work as a designer of lettering, title pages, covers, whatnot. Times for us were hard—commissions were few and a son was born. We weathered the storms—that is, we still existed. Frank Holme, a newspaper artist, started his School of Illustration and asked me to conduct a class in lettering and design. I kept one lesson ahead of my pupils, but Frank was generous and pretended that my work was satisfactory. Through him I met Wm. Jean Beauley, an architect, who was in charge of the advertising art work for Hart, Schaffner & Marx. Mr. Beauley gave me considerable work to do for his firm. He was a severe taskmaster but a generous one. Then Waldo P. Warren, advertising manager for Marshall Field & Company, appeared on the scene with more work and things became easier. Orders for title pages and covers for McClurg's and other publishers were frequent.

 I had become acquainted by this time (1901-3) with Mr. Weinstock, the advertising manager for Kuppenheimer & Company, and he invited me to make a type

The Village Press: An Introduction

design for the use of his firm. In a little monograph* published by the present publishers of this rambling account, I told the history of this type and quote a part of that story here, since the designing of that type played a large part in the founding of The Village Press.

"The commission to do a type for Kuppenheimer was welcome, and I began the work, basing my forms more or less on the types of Jenson as exhibited in Morris's Golden type, in the Doves, Montaigne, Merrymount, and types of that ilk. What an ancestry for an advertising display face!

"In due time the drawings were completed, submitted to Mr. Weinstock and thoroughly approved by him. The question then arose regarding the cost of producing matrices from which to cast type in various sizes for the use of the clothing firm, and while the figure quoted by the matrix cutter was less than half the cost of similar work today, the total cost seemed too great for the treasurer of the clothing firm who probably figured he was 'buying a pig in a poke' anyway. After discussing ways and means with Mr. Weinstock,

---

**The Story of the Village Type*, by Frederic W. Goudy. Published 1933 by the Press of the Woolly Whale, New York.

the firm finally decided to pay me a nominal sum for my time and return the drawings to me.

"So ended the first chapter. As I look back upon the matter now, I have serious doubt that the design would have proved an advertising success, except as far as the novelty of the idea was concerned. However, it was more or less a courageous gesture on Kuppenheimer's part to go even as far as they did. The type matter closed, I took up my routine of work; book covers, title pages, initial letters, borders, headbands, advertisements, etc., as commissions offered. In the spring of 1903, 'a wildly enthusiastic youngster' from Snohomish, Washington, who was studying at the Art Institute in Chicago, asked permission to work under and with me in my shop in the Fine Arts Building. This 'youngster,' Will Ransom, had done some book printing of a minor sort before migrating East and there remained with him the desire and enthusiasm to engage again in producing books. As I recall it, Ransom was working with me at the time I was designing the type for Kuppenheimer & Company and I imagine that since a nucleus for a private press was presented by the repossession of the design, that fact had much to do with our decision to establish a press.

The Village Press: An Introduction

Nevertheless, many were the discussions of various details before the step finally was taken. Of course a name for the new venture was necessary. Looking about for suitable matter for reprint, I recall that I came across the poem *The Village Blacksmith* and as we—Mrs. Goudy and I—were living in the Village of Park Ridge, Illinois (a suburb of Chicago), the thought came to me 'why not The Village Press?' The suggestion met with Ransom's approval and the new-born Press was christened. Roswell Field, brother of Eugene Field, and himself a writer, later told me 'the name was a real inspiration.'"

I want to speak here of an incident that occurred but a few months ago. When the Ulster-Irish Society of New York on March 19, 1937, kindly gave their fifth medal to me for typographic creations, and which was presented by Madame Frances Perkins, Secretary of Labor, the Society presented to her at the same time a copy of the first Village Press publication—*Printing*, by William Morris. When some days later she came to visit me at Deepdene, she brought along this copy of *Printing*, which she asked me to autograph for her. I was interested to note that the book bore the bookplate and autograph of its former owner, Roswell

The Village Press: An Introduction

Field. A private price mark showed that it came to him from A. C. McClurg & Co., to whom several copies had been sold. The book itself turned up in the bookshop of my friend Duschnes of New York, but through how many hands it had passed since 1903 I have no idea. It was in the original protective case and in "mint" condition. I am glad it again has a good home with an appreciative owner.

Will Ransom, in his excellent *Private Presses and their Books*, has this to say:

"The Village Press began its existence in the summer of 1903, the first proof having been pulled on July 17th. But before the press was the type. In fact, the press came into being because of the type. Where William Morris approached type design through making illuminated manuscripts in mediæval hands, Mr. Goudy was at that time and for many subsequent years in the full swing of drawing modern letters for advertising matter. The result was that the Village type contained elements of drawing, subtle curves and delicate joinings, fresh and new and strangely interesting. It was not definitely copied from nor based upon any previous letter, though it had something of a fifteenth century Italian air about it. One essence it had was in

The Village Press: An Introduction

being drawn entirely freehand, a startling innovation in those days when mechanical accuracy was the *sine que non* of all type, at least in this country."*

As I wrote in my story of the Village type:

"The type already drawn for one purpose was now to be devoted to another; its humble beginnings must be ignored and as a private press type it must be fitted with a halo and supplied with a more glamorous aspect with no taint of vulgar trade ancestry.

"The first announcement of the Press regarding the type bears, then, a mild departure from the actual facts, although a few minor changes were made in the final design before cutting to warrant, somewhat, the statements made therein. Quoting the announcement: 'The Village type was designed by Mr. Goudy for the exclusive use of the Press.... The design seems based on an early Italian model but Mr. Goudy disclaims any conscious intention of imitation, rather having evolved letter by letter gradually as ideas came, taking some of the best modern faces—the Golden of Morris, the Montaigne of Bruce Rogers, the Merrymount of B. G. Goodhue, the Doves of Emery

* All of the types drawn since the Village, nearly a hundred in number, have been drawn freehand.—F. W. G.

Walker, with critical and careful consideration of many others—selecting and adopting those points in each which appealed to him, making changes, and with one idea firmly in mind throughout, that of considering each letter as being a pen-letter reduced to type with all its limitations of material and use as type.'

"The drawings for the type were made about three-fourths of an inch in height. As it was my first attempt at a book face, I did not know that the type cutter would find it necessary to make large patterns from my drawings and that the type itself might lose somewhat in the reproduction, since it is practically impossible for one draughtsman to retain every quality of a drawing made by another, otherwise I should have made drawings the same size as the required patterns as I later did for other types cut for me.

"The drawings for the type, after a few slight revisions, were entrusted to the late Robert Wiebking of Chicago who interpreted them faithfully, although 'frankly shocked at some of the liberties' I had taken with a few letters, liberties which did not meet with his entire approval. The size decided upon was 16 pt., and 150 pounds of type were cast by Mr. Wiebking for our use from the matrices engraved by him. I desire here to acknowledge my gratitude to Mr. Wiebking for his help and forbearance which, in my early days of inexperience, he invariably and ungrudgingly gave me. I am proud of the friendship that existed for over a quarter century."

Morris, Cobden-Sanderson, St. John Hornby, all availed themselves of the services of Edward Prince, dean of English punch cutters, for the cutting of their types; he cut punches and made drives from them. For the Village type, the matrices were engraved direct pantagraphically in steel from patterns made from my drawings. Only two or three letters were recut. St. John Hornby speaks of the endless discussions he had with Sydney Cockerell, who had been Secretary to the Kelmscott Press, and Sir Emery Walker, and "the omniscient Robert Procter" of the British Museum, regarding the Subiaco type he was about to have cut, and tells how proud he was when he received the first trial letters. Alas, we had no such coterie of typographic learning to consult, but I do not believe St. John Hornby experienced any greater pleasure than was ours at the first sight of the Village characters actually in metal types.

The type cut, cast and laid in our cases, the next

step was the press and equipment with which to give our efforts visible form. After much shopping around we selected a Schneidewend & Lee proof press; I forget the maker's official designation as to size, but I recall that the platen was about 14 x 19 inches. One thing we wanted with it which ordinarily would not be supplied was a frisket, the frame attached to the tympan which protects the sheet to be printed from smudging of ink that gets on the furniture, etc. This the makers kindly added and, as I remember, without charge. The press was installed and then began a search for ink suitable for hand-press work on dampened handmade papers. The hand-press tradition had almost disappeared in 1903—inks were made for fast-moving power presses, not the laborious and slow hand-presses, and the ink-makers I called on with our problem seemed as ignorant as we ourselves as to our requirements. Finally, and almost by accident, I found a dealer who sold me a can of Jaenecke ink imported from Germany. The first impressions from our new type had been disappointing—with a page of the Doves Press edition of *The Ideal Book* before us for comparison we couldn't even approximate the quality of its impression. What was the trouble? Is it ignorance of press technique or what? We tried various inks with indifferent success; we could not get the sharp, clean impression, even color, try as we might. The first attempt with the newly acquired Jaenecke ink convinced us that poor ink rather than our own press shortcomings was to blame. The new ink had color, density and distributed evenly; we found later that we could get a better quality of the same black—one with a better grade of pigment, combined with just enough varnish to hold it and properly ground in oil. Much of our trouble was thus overcome, although we still had much to learn—the correct damping of papers, as each different sort seemed to require its own peculiar handling, was difficult to master. It was necessary to "back up" sheets printed on one side while the paper was still damp in order to secure evenness of color; if attempted too soon, too much "set-off" would occur, the impression would be fuzzy, and if too much time was allowed before backing up, paper would shrink and register would be impossible. Experience here was our only teacher. Another thing we had to learn was the use of bearers to carry portions of the impression when the form was unequally paged and not show marks of the bearers on the printed sheets, and many other points that came up with each new production.

The press, while powerful and exact, was not primarily built for fine book work. It really was only a glorified Washington hand press for newspaper use. The impression could be regulated somewhat by a wedge that increased or lightened the pressure of the platen on the paper, but it lacked the impression screws of my modern Albion, which will permit giving a different degree of pressure on each of the four quarters of the platen, a feature especially valuable when printing a form, say, of four pages—of which one page may contain only a few lines, thus receiving too heavy pressure of that page. By backing off on the impression screw controlling the impression for that portion of the form and screwing down on the others, the excess pressure is lightened.

We learned too that the stiff ink required a roller with suction, and such rollers seemed particularly susceptible to variations of humidity. On a humid day, the roller would simply refuse to accept a coating of ink or transfer what it did accept to the type; because of the absorbed moisture it would not affiliate with the oily ink.

The Village Press: An Introduction

Gradually these things were learned and work became easier although no amount of acquired knowledge of details eliminated the brute force required to pull the bar on a heavy form. Yet even here a certain "knack" did develop that enabled me to pull heavy impressions more or less easily, although a much stronger person than I without the "knack" would find the same pull difficult if not almost impossible to perform.

Bertha liked to tell of an incident which amused her greatly. One hot day in August I was pulling sheets of *Printing*—Ransom probably was inking the form; my hands were moist with perspiration and the pull heavy, my hands slipped off the bar at the extreme point of the impression, I went backwards through the double doorway of the barn, which at first housed the press and equipment, the bar flew back because of the heavy springs which lifted the platen after the impression and the jar dislodged the toggle, parts of the toggle scattered in all directions, and for a moment we were fearful that the whole thing was busted and rendered useless. The thing that amused her was the sight of me on my back, legs in the air, wildly struggling to right myself to see just what really had happened. Luckily, only my sense of dignity suffered, the

The Village Press: An Introduction

parts of the press were replaced and everything went on as though nothing had happened. Thirty-four years ago I, of course, was not the dignified, white-haired old gentleman of today; just think—on second thought, don't think—of the shock to my *amour propre* if something like that should happen now!

On another occasion, some boys from the neighborhood stopped by to see us at work on the press. One of them, more curious than the others, asked me what type metal was. I told him it was "an alloy of lead, tin and antimony." A few minutes later another boy, a friend of those already in the shop, came in. Immediately he was hailed with "you don't know what type metal is." He acknowledged his ignorance, but intimated that neither did his interrogator, who replied quickly, "I do too; it's lead, and tin, and alimony."

The first paper we used was obtained from the Japan Paper Company of New York. It was called "Alton Mill" and made in England. It was not a good paper in some ways—one, in the matter of sizing and when dampened it gave off an unpleasant odor; it printed pretty well when we got on to its idiosyncrasies. We had much better luck with a small sheet of Whatman, another English paper, which I found at an

The Village Press: An Introduction

art store; it was whiter and stronger sized. We could get a sheet that seemed to suit *The Hollow Land* layout—or maybe we made *The Hollow Land* layout to fit the paper, I don't recall—anyway it was quite satisfactory for hand-press work. *The Blessed Damozel* was done on Japan Vellum; the day we printed the sheets everything worked beautifully, good register, good color, and I remember we—Bertha and I—worked off the greatest number of impressions we ever accomplished, 160 an hour. The old hand-press printers used to consider a "token" an hour, 250 pulls, as the proper number, but ours were more carefully executed than most of the old work.

Occasionally we used Van Gelder, a Dutch paper, but it often varied as to thickness, some sheets thin in one part and thicker in another, and usually sheets even of different thicknesses in the same ream. Later we used Hammer and Anvil, made by Batchelor & Sons, Little Chart, England, who made this paper first for William Morris. This in two sizes proved the best for our work.

Now in the face of all that has been written of the work of The Village Press, I maintain still that, except from a sentimental standpoint the books we issued,

The Village Press: An Introduction

while interesting to us or to indulgent friends, are not such as deserve a bibliography, unless some ground other than a consideration of them as examples of fine printing may be found. What do we find?

Here I am moved to quote again from my friend Ransom in the hope that a reason may be turned up. He says:

"The Village Press is 'the outward and visible sign of an inward and spiritual grace' immanent in two remarkable personalities, Frederic and Bertha Goudy, and the history of the Press is a record of one portion of their abilities, activities, and achievements, elements which have made its output both intensely interesting and genuinely influential."

And here I must say something of that other member of the Press, Bertha M. Goudy, to whose deft craftsmanship and rare natural aptitude for type composition any excellences of the books of the Press are due. Without her help, her enthusiasm and patience, her craftsmanship, the probability is that after the early retirement of my associate Will Ransom, the Press undoubtedly would almost have died a-borning. Ransom himself says of her:

"Not least among the intangibles, as well as the

The Village Press: An Introduction

achievements of The Village Press, are the spirit and performance of Bertha Goudy. From the installation of the first equipment she manifested not only a keen interest in technical processes, but also a marked ability in craftsmanship. It was this writer's privilege to initiate her into the 'art and mystery of printing,' if one may be said to lead a pupil whose instinctive grasp of details outruns instruction before the lesson is finished."

The books and printed work hereinafter tabulated do, in fact, represent a sincere and painstaking effort toward simplicity and dignity. The earlier productions are not examples of rare literary value or of selections little known; too frequently they were selected because copyright had expired or they were otherwise available, or more probably because the matter seemed to offer opportunities for distinctive treatment. The first book, *Printing*, was intended as a tribute and acknowledgment of obligation to William Morris; the second, *The Blessed Damozel*, because my friend Clarence Marder (who years before had purchased my earliest designs for the type foundry) wanted something to give a few friends for a Christmas greeting, and he selected the poem of which 110 copies were

The Village Press: An Introduction

made, taking 50 copies; the remaining copies we offered for sale. The third, *The Hollow Land,* was undertaken primarily because Mr. Millard of McClurg's was kind enough to lend us the bound volume of the rare *Oxford & Cambridge Magazine* in which Morris's story first appeared—and so on.

A celebrated surgeon was once complimented upon the celerity with which he performed an operation for cataract. His reply was, "Yes, I can operate quickly, but I spoiled a bushel of eyes learning how to do it so quickly." Many of our productions were the "eyes" on which we attempted to learn private pressing. There would be little point in detailing all the incidents relating to each item even if I could remember them. Whenever anything seems worthy of special note, I have attempted to include it in the account of that particular item in the bibliography.

19  03

THE FIRST DAYS OF
THE VILLAGE PRESS
Extracts from the Diary of
WILL RANSOM

Monday, March 16th. Saturday morning went down to hunt up W. Irving Way. Found him out—Goudy in, who spotted me for "the man from Snohomish." He is very pleasant and treated me extremely well.

Friday, March 27th. This noon I left the Art Institute a bit early and hunted up Goudy. Went to lunch with him, the young fellow that works with him, and Oswald Cooper, teacher in the Frank Holme Correspondence School. After lunch Goudy took me into McClurg's and showed me several fine bindings and a couple of illuminated manuscript books. Had a fine talk with him.

Saturday, April 4th. Before I went to work this morning I went up to see Goudy and he made me a proposition to work with him during the summer. I might make enough to live on, but probably not, and then he may go East within the next sixty days, so that the whole thing is up in the air just at present. However, if circumstances permit, I shall make an awful effort to make it stick. Goudy has been exceptionally nice to me since I came, and if things turn out as I wish I will be indebted to him beyond all hope of repayment.

Monday, April 13th. Saturday afternoon I spent with Goudy, reading Brown's *Letters and Lettering* most of the time.

Monday, April 20th. Decided to go over to Goudy's when my time is out at the Institute and stay with it as long as I can. It will probably mean that I will have to work next year, but what experience I get will be valuable.

Sunday, May 24th. Last Thursday, the 21st, I left the Institute and for the summer shall spend all my time with Goudy. He is planning to put in a press and turn most of his attention to bookmaking, and wants me to work with him. He has designed a remarkably good face of type, but we haven't either of us enough money to get that cut and get the plant too, so we are just now figuring on ways and means. It will all come

The Village Press: The First Days

around some way, but it is none too clear just now. I wrote Jack Bird last night to see if he has any idle money he is willing to loan me, for if I can get hold of some I can get a half interest in the proposition, which would suit me much better than letting Goudy buy everything and then being under obligation to him for letting me use it. However, I have no occasion to speak of the affair, for the whole thing is entirely in the air, and there is nothing at all definite to tell.

Saturday, June 6th. Heard from Jack Bird the other day and, while he has no idle money of his own, he offers to help me get some, and on the strength of that Goudy and I went out to Wiebking's Thursday afternoon, the 4th day in June, and ordered the cutting of the new type. That will probably take at least a month, and by that time we hope to have the press in, the Shop arranged, and most of the material on hand to go right to work. Yesterday I began cutting on the wood the initial "A" for the announcement of the type and the founding of the Press, which will be the first job. Finished the initial block today, but spoiled the decoration block and will have to cut another one. Goudy designed a little band to be used on the first announcement this afternoon, and I will put that on the wood and begin cutting it as soon as I get the initial done.

Friday, July 3rd. Here am I at Park Ridge, but for a few days entirely at liberty, for the type is not yet finished and all my drawing materials are at the office yet, so I can't work at any of mine own stunts. Since my last writing I have cut the band for the first announcement and the one for the title page of *Printing.* Wednesday we got a proof of the lower-case characters, hand-cast on an eighteen point body.

Sunday, July 12th. Didn't get any word from Jack Bird in response to the note, so finally appealed to Jas. Moore, and his brother, of the Cedar Rapids Savings Bank, advanced $250 on my two insurance policies. That money came last Wednesday morning and that day Fred and I went and bought the press and made a payment on the American Type Founders bill. Perkins, the expressman, brought all the stuff (except the type) out Friday, but did not deliver it here until Saturday morning. Fred and I worked until nearly one o'clock, unpacking and setting things up. Got most of it done, and as soon as we get a few small things will be ready to go to work in earnest as soon as the type comes, which may be Tuesday. The barn promises to make a very convenient and comfortable shop.

The Village Press: The First Days

Thursday, July 23rd. At last we have begun actual work in the Shop. Although a couple of the characters were not here yet, Fred set the first circular Sunday. I was sick all that day and was hardly off the bed. Was all right again Monday and cleaned up around the Shop and got No. 1 onto the press. Mrs. G. went to town with Fred to get the commas and some spaces.

The type finally all arrived Monday night and Tuesday morning we went to press with the first circular. The tympan and frisket sheets gave us a great deal of trouble on account of the paper not being stretched properly, and the ink, for a part of the time, refused to work at all, so that we had a pretty hard time of it and made poor work of the circular. We made about 90 impressions and numbered and issued the first 14—1 and 2 on vellum, 3-8 inclusive on Japan Vellum, 9-14 inclusive on Whatman. Shall send an extra unnumbered one to K— and keep another extra unnumbered one with my vellum and JV copies. Decided to reprint the whole thing on Alton Mills handmade and that is on the press now, ready to be run first thing in the morning.

Yesterday afternoon we ran off some of the envelopes, and a lot more today, and followed them with some letterheads. Mrs. G. helped me with the presswork today and Fred set the latter part of No. 2, which Mrs. G. had begun. Started to fuss with the order blank this afternoon, but didn't make anything out of it so far.

Tuesday, July 28th. We did the order blank the next day. Saturday I set the first three pages of *Printing*, but had to stop then because the lowercase "i's" gave out. We didn't get the right proportion of "i's" in the first place—the other letters are holding out well. Wiebking agreed to send some down to Fred yesterday, but they didn't show up. Yesterday morning we started to do the presswork on No. 2 but the roller was green, the ink heavy, and the atmosphere muddy, so we couldn't do a thing with it. Worked at it all the morning, but with poor success. Tried it again this morning but, while the ink worked fairly well, the paper was too damp to take a good impression.

Sunday, August 16th. Things have been going so utterly bad at the Shop that I haven't felt a bit like writing about it. We labored over No. 2, tried some new inks, and finally ran it on the 8th, 9th and 10th of this month, using some ink that we got from Hellmuth. However, it wasn't the right ink, and the circulars seem worse every time we look at them, so that we have been getting bluer and bluer. But yesterday afternoon Fred brought home some of Jaenecke's "Heavy Black" lithographic ink, and it is so much better that we begin to feel better again. We have gotten some really good prints last night and today, but the ink seems not to have the rich black color we would like. We shall go ahead and use it for *Printing* and also for the *Roast Pig* unless we find something better before that. Clarence Collins Marder was out here for dinner today and we made a few proofs of the *Ideal Book* quotation. We will arrange that matter, put a woodcut initial on it, and send them out as souvenirs. We plan to do several little stunts like that. After the No. 2 was run it gave me some type to work with, so I have been pretty busy this week. When I got that thrown in I finished the 10th page of *Printing*, set a little page of Latin to see how the type looked in that and also as a trial page for the *Roast Pig*, set and printed a *To the Trade* circular and order form for *Printing*, set an ad for *The Printing Art*, which we probably will not use after all, and set some of *The Deserted Village* to figure on page sizes with. Threw in that last again this morning to get type for *The Ideal Book*.

The Village Press: The First Days

Monday, August 17th. Began cutting block No. 4 this morning, but quit at 11 o'clock and put the title page to *Printing* on the press and Mrs. Goudy and I ran the black this afternoon. Used the new ink (Jaenecke's) with very good results. Hope to do the red tomorrow.

Saturday, August 22nd. We had no red ink here, so Tuesday morning I went down town, got some, and hurried back. Mrs. G. was gone both Tuesday and Wednesday. Finished cutting block No. 4 and ran the red on the title page Tuesday afternoon. We planned to do the black on the first form Thursday afternoon and Fred came home early, but the paper was not soft enough, so we had to redampen it and run them Friday morning. Mrs. G. and I put the red on in the afternoon, and I distributed all of the first form except page 3, which we are going to use for a specimen page. This morning I put the second form on the press (pp. 4, 5, 8, 9) and dampened the stock, and we hope to run that tomorrow.

Tuesday, September 15th. I don't remember now whether we ran them the next day, but they are done now, as are also the remaining pages, and the books are all sewed and glued. Today we completed the first copy (No. 231) but didn't do any more, as the card-

The Village Press: The First Days

board for the covers is not here yet and we had to use Strathmore for the one we did. Fred brought a few sheets of cover stock last night, so I expect to do a few books tomorrow, although he will not be able to be here.

Wednesday, September 16th. Have been binding all day and did nine books. Fred plans to stay tomorrow and we hope to do several.

Saturday, September 26th. Started composition on *The Hollow Land* yesterday and Mrs. G. put in yesterday afternoon and a couple of hours today. I have been doing odd ...

(*All succeeding pages torn out—reason unknown*)

A BIBLIOGRAPHY OF THE VILLAGE PRESS

BERTHA M. GOUDY
(PHOTO BY EARL H. EMMONS)

1903  1938

A BIBLIOGRAPHY OF
THE VILLAGE PRESS
Compiled by
MELBERT B. CARY, JR.

It is fitting that the thirty-fifth anniversary of the oldest private press in the United States should be marked by a bibliography of its accomplishments.

Thirty-five years is a long time for such an essentially personal enterprise as a private press to endure. The Kelmscott Press ceased after only seven years, though in this brief period William Morris not only printed, but sold, the surprising total of 53 titles (one in eight volumes), besides issuing 64 minor pieces sufficiently important to be enumerated in the final volume issued after his death. A closer parallel is found in the distinguished career of the Ashendene Press. Its first book appeared in 1895, eight years before The Village Press was founded. In its fortieth volume, a sumptuous review of its 40 years of accomplishment issued in 1935, Mr. C. H. St. John Hornby brought its work to a dignified and distinguished conclusion. Besides the 23 minor pieces which he catalogs, many others must have been issued.

Nineteen hundred thirty-eight marks the completion of the thirty-fifth year of The Village Press. Its activities may be seen in detail in the bibliography which follows. Inevitably there have been periods of greater or less activity, but at no time, except perhaps at the very outset, has The Village Press been the sole, or even the principal, employment of its owner. Its publications, numerous though they seem in retrospect, must be viewed as the running accompaniment of Mr. Goudy's varied activities as designer, author and typefounder.

It has been a temptation to include in this bibliography much material relating to Mr. Goudy's kindred interests—material that is not strictly germane to The Village Press. A successful resistance has resulted in the exclusion of all reference to Mr. Goudy's earlier work as a designer and calligrapher, and to his later contributions in the field of type. No mention, likewise, is possible of his first quasi-commercial experiment in printing, the Booklet Press, later the Camelot

Press, happily described in his introduction, or to his activities as editor of such diverse periodicals as *Modern Advertising* and the *American Cat News*.

Instead, it has been necessary to limit the following list to work actually done at The Village Press. Even this decision has necessitated qualification, for in numerous cases, especially in recent years, books have been executed partially at The Village Press and completed elsewhere, and vice versa. Particularly since the sale of its power press, Mr. Goudy has frequently entrusted to others the actual printing of text which Mrs. Goudy had composed and the typography of which he had designed.

It has accordingly seemed wise to include in the following bibliography all items on which the composition or the presswork (or both) have been done at The Village Press and to exclude such other items as have merely been designed by Mr. Goudy and executed elsewhere, or for which he has supplied decorative material. A permissible exception to this rule is found in the inclusion of the first volume of *Ars Typographica*. The importance of Mr. Goudy's contribution as editor and publisher of this magazine is so great, that failure to list it here would constitute a serious omission, even though only a fraction of the total composition and presswork was actually performed at the Press.

Because some of the incidental, smaller items from The Village Press are among the most interesting and typographically varied (as well as the rarest), these fugitive pieces are included with brief comment. The formal books are more completely described, but the laborious minutiæ of collation, appropriate to rare incunabula, have been here omitted in favor of a simpler and more practical system of description.

The arrangement is strictly chronological, from the first work issued by the Press in 1903 through 1937, each item numbered consecutively. In each year the bound books have arbitrarily been placed first in the order of their appearance, followed by the ephemera of that year. The sizes are based on the page, not the binding.

All this is as might be expected. The unusual and invaluable feature of this bibliography is the comment accompanying many items. For it has been possible to add frequent illuminating bits of personal reminiscence, supplied by Mr. Goudy himself—statements which shed a warm glow of human interest over each inanimate book, and enable us to share, at least in some degree, in the hopes, the disappointments and the enthusiasm that accompanied the making of each volume. If this purpose is accomplished, the compiler will feel content.

THE FIRST MARK OF THE VILLAGE PRESS

THE FIRST SITE OF THE VILLAGE PRESS,
PARK RIDGE, ILLINOIS
(PHOTO BY PHILIP G. REED)

PUBLICATIONS OF THE VILLAGE PRESS
AT PARK RIDGE, ILLINOIS
1903  1904

1. Printing

PRINTING [*in red*] | AN ESSAY BY WILLIAM MORRIS & EMERY | WALKER. FROM "ARTS & CRAFTS ES-SAYS | BY MEMBERS OF THE ARTS AND CRAFTS | EXHIBITION SOCIETY" | [*Fleuron, in red*] | PARK RIDGE | THE VILLAGE PRESS | M·CM·III

COLOPHON: Here ends *Printing*, an essay by William Morris and Emery Walker, reprinted from *Arts and Crafts Essays by Members of the Arts and Crafts Exhibition Society*. Designed, printed in the Village type, and bound by Fred. W. Goudy and Will H. Ransom at the Village Press, Park Ridge, Illinois, in the month of August, 1903. Of 231 copies, (200 for sale), this is number — Published & for sale by the Village Press.

PAGES: [6]+16+[6]. Size 7 x 9¼ inches.

DESIGNS: The word PRINTING, fleuron on title page and 11-line initial 'P' on first page of text drawn by F. W. Goudy, as is the tailpiece which is present on

1903 page 16 on some copies, omitted on others. The press mark is the first designed (reproduced on page 49) and was used on no other book.

BINDING: Boards covered with brown laid paper. Title printed in red on side. Slip case.

EDITION: 231 numbered copies, on Alton Mill; 200 for sale at $3. Village type. Ransom No. 1.

COMMENT: The first book issued by The Village Press and the first composed in the Village type. Exhibited at the Louisiana Purchase Exposition at St. Louis, 1904.

2. [A Book for a Wedding]

Ransom No. 2.

"My recollection of this volume is hazy and I have no proofs. It was either a collection of poems for a gift, or a record of the ceremony, including letters, etc. I think it was the former.

"The size may have been a foolscap quarto on Whatman. I am quite sure that the pages were ruled by hand in red and that the initials were drawn in. It was bound in limp parchment or vellum. One copy only was printed in August or September."

—Will Ransom.

"I think this was printed on Whatman, for Edgar Bancroft of Chicago."—F. W. G.

1903

3. The Blessed Damozel

THE | BLESSED DAMOZEL · A POEM | by DANTE GABRIEL ROSSETTI | REPRINTED FROM THE GERM · | [*Floral Band*]

COLOPHON: Here ends *The Blessed Damozel* by Dante Gabriel Rossetti; reprinted from *The Germ* for February M·DCCC·L. Printed & bound by Fred W. and Bertha M. Goudy at the Village Press. 110 copies printed, 98 for sale. Park Ridge, Illinois, December, 1903.

PAGES: [8] + [18 *unnumbered*] + [6]. Size 4⅝ x 6¼ inches.

DESIGNS: Two photogravure reproductions, the frontispiece a portrait of Rossetti by G. F. Watts; also *The Blessed Damozel* by Rossetti. Floral band on title page and initial 'T' in red drawn by F. W. Goudy. The press mark is the second designed, its first use.

BINDING: Limp parchment, sewed with green silk. Some with stiff covers and two green silk ties.

EDITION: 110 copies on Japan Vellum, 50 for Clarence Marder, 48 for sale at $1.50. Village type. Ransom No. 3.

1903 COMMENT: Reprinted from *The Germ* of February, 1850. The form containing the red initial 'T' was printed by Bertha M. Goudy. Exhibited at the Louisiana Purchase Exposition, St. Louis, 1904. Reported out of print in March, 1904 (Announcement No. 6).

THE SECOND MARK OF THE VILLAGE PRESS

Fugitive Items

4. FRED W. GOUDY AND WILL H. RANSOM

Announcement No. 1; four-page folder, 7 x 9 inches, in black and red. Decorative headband and 8-line initial 'T' in red, designed by F. W. Goudy and cut on wood by Will H. Ransom. About 90 numbered copies, 1 and 2 on vellum, 3-8 inclusive on Japanese Vellum, 9-14 inclusive on Whatman, and the balance on Alton Mill. July 24.

A Bibliography of The Village Press

5. To THE VILLAGE PRESS, PARK RIDGE, ILLINOIS, 1903. **1903**
Order blank for *Printing*. Bond paper, 5 x 3¼ inches. Six lines in Village type, printed in red ink; July 24.

6. A NOTE ON THE VILLAGE PRESS AND TYPE
Announcement No. 2; four-page folder, 7 x 9 inches, in black and red. Headband as in No. 1, and 8-line initial 'A' cut on wood by Will H. Ransom. Only use of first press mark in two colors. Alton Mill. July 28.

7. VIATORES TRES ITINERE
Eighteen lines of Latin in Village type, on a single leaf of hand-made paper, 4 x 7½ inches. August 12.

8. [The FIRST ADVERTISEMENT of THE VILLAGE PRESS]
In *The Dial* of September 16, 1903.

9. THE IDEAL BOOK
Leaf of Alton Mill, 7 x 9 inches, containing quotation from T. J. Cobden-Sanderson in 16 lines. Initial by Will Ransom. Sixty copies were printed as souvenirs for a little group that came to visit the Press one Sunday, August 16. Ransom No. B-1.

10. BOOKS FOR SALE AND IN PREPARATION
Announcement No. 3. Four-page folder on Alton Mill, 7 x 9 inches, in black. 160 copies, September 2.

1903 11. BOOKS FOR SALE AND IN PREPARATION
Announcement No. 4. Four-page folder on Whatman, 7 x 8¼ inches, in black. Contains a specimen page of *The Hollow Land* and lists four books as ready, in the press or in preparation. September 29.

12. BOOKS FOR SALE AND IN PREPARATION
Announcement No. 5. Four-page folder on Whatman, 6¾ x 8¼ inches, in black and red. 12-line, 2-color initial 'P,' the same used on first text page of *Printing*, but colors reversed. Also fleuron used as tailpiece on some copies of *Printing*. First use of the second press mark on an announcement.

The Village Press gives notice of its purchase of the interest of Will H. Ransom. November 6.

13. A Dissertation Upon Roast Pig

1904 A DIS- | SERTA- | TION | UPON | ROAST | PIG | One of the | ESSAYS | of ELIA | With a Note on | LAMB'S LITER- | ARY MOTIVE | by Cyrus Lauron | Hooper

Colophon: Here ends *A Dissertation upon Roast Pig* by Charles Lamb, one of the essays which first appeared in the *London Magazine* under the name of Elia and here reprinted from the first edition (1823) with an introduction on *Lamb's Literary Motive* by Cyrus

Lauron Hooper. Printed in the Village type at The Village Press, Park Ridge, Illinois, by Fred W. & Bertha M. Goudy, and finished February 29, 1904 — the third book issued from the Press. 1904

PAGES: [10]+52+[10]. Size 4⅝ x 6¼ inches.

DESIGNS: Five floral bands, two all-around page borders (used twice), 7-line initial 'T' and 5-line initial 'M,' all by F. W. Goudy. First use of monogram 'TVP' as tailpiece on page 24. Second press mark.

THE FIRST VILLAGE PRESS MONOGRAM

BINDING: Gray boards, with parchment back, gold lettered. A few copies bound in parchment over flexible boards, with green silk ties.

EDITION: 215 copies on Imperial Japanese Vellum, 200 for sale at $3. Village type. Ransom No. 4.

COMMENT: Mr. Goudy relates that the first design for the first text page commencing 'Mankind' originally included an initial 'M' unlike that subsequently used and considerably larger, and entirely lacked the all-around border finally adopted.

1904 When set, the completed page did not seem to match properly with the title page opposite, and he accordingly designed a new initial 'M' and decided to repeat the all-around border on both pages. Meantime, the reverse of the signature had already been printed.

When the work was done Mr. Goudy suddenly realized that the page as redesigned might not accommodate exactly the amount of text originally allotted to it—an essential, since the following page had already been printed. To his astonishment and delight, however, he found upon resetting the first page that it accommodated exactly the words which had to be squeezed into it.

Mr. Goudy further reports that the book contains an inverted 's,' which he has never been able to find since it was first pointed out to him. This book was exhibited at the Louisiana Purchase Exposition, St. Louis, 1904. Probably some 50 copies were destroyed in the Parker Building fire, 1908.

14. The Blind Princess and the Dawn

THE BLIND PRINCESS AND | THE DAWN. TWO POEMS

PAGES: Probably 12, about 6¾ x 8½ inches.

DESIGNS: Initials and decorations drawn in by F. W. Goudy.   **1904**

BINDING: Parchment.

EDITION: Only one copy printed, on Whatman, for John Weber Linn. Village type. February.

Fugitive Item

15. THE VILLAGE PRESS PUBLICATIONS

Announcement No. 6. Four-page leaflet, French fold, 4½ x 6⅛ inches. Composed in Village type. The border on page one is that used on *A Dissertation Upon Roast Pig*. Announces that *The Blessed Damozel* is out of print. Park Ridge, Ill. March.

THE PRESS OCCUPIED THE GROUND FLOOR ROOM
TO THE RIGHT OF THE FRONT DOOR
LINCOLN STREET, HINGHAM, MASSACHUSETTS

PUBLICATIONS OF THE VILLAGE PRESS
AT HINGHAM, MASSACHUSETTS
1904  1906

16. The Ninety-First Psalm

THE | NINETY-FIRST PSALM [*in red*] | FROM THE TEXT OF THE | AUTHORIZED VERSION | OF THE ENGLISH BIBLE | [3 *fleurons in red*]

COLOPHON: Psalm Ninety-First, here reprinted from the text of the Authorized Version of the English Bible, by Fred W. and Bertha M. Goudy, The Village Press, October, 1904. Sold at The Village Press, Hingham, Massachusetts.

PAGES: [6] + [19 *unnumbered*] + [7]. Size 3½ x 4½ inches.

DESIGNS: 12-line initial 'H' in red. Monogram 'TVP' on half title.

BINDING: White boards, title in red on side.

EDITION: 200 numbered copies on Alton Mill at $1. Village type. Ransom No. 5.

COMMENT: When printed this little booklet made such a slight volume that it was decided not to bind

1904 it. But visitors to the Press asked for copies. Accordingly it was bound and at $1 apiece sold more than other books. Copies were sent without thought of selling any to an exposition being held by the Arts and Crafts Society, but some 30 to 40 copies were taken.

17. Rabbi Ben Ezra

RABBI | BEN EZRA | A DRAMATIC MONOLOGUE | BY ROBERT BROWNING | [*ornament in red*]

COLOPHON: Here ends *Rabbi Ben Ezra,* a Dramatic Monologue written by Robert Browning, with a note by Robert Bruere. Printed by hand at The Village Press, Hingham, Massachusetts, by Fred and Bertha Goudy. Frontispiece and decorations designed & cut on wood by Will Dwiggins. One hundred seventy three copies printed, November 1904. For sale at The Village Press.

PAGES: [6]+[27 *unnumbered*]+[7]. Size 5x8 inches.

DESIGNS: Frontispiece, title and tailpiece in black; decoration and 9-line initial 'G' in red by W. A. Dwiggins, who writes of them: "I think the picture was my third attempt to make a woodcut. It was, as you say, cut with a knife on the side of the plank, in the Oriental way, through a drawing pasted down on the wood.

The red vine-business on the title page was a wood- 1904
cut, too..." Second press mark.

BINDING: Gray boards, parchment back lettered in red.

EDITION: 173 numbered copies on Arches at $2, plus 2 or 3 on Japan Vellum. Village type. Ransom No. 6.

18. Good King Wenceslas

GOOD KING | WENCESLAS | A CAROL WRITTEN | BY DR NEALE · PIC | TURES BY ARTHUR | GASKIN · WITH AN | INTRODUCTION BY | WILLIAM MORRIS | HINGHAM · MASSACHUSETTS | M · CM · IV

COLOPHON: Reprinted from the edition issued by Cornish Brothers. Double border and title from drawings by Will Dwiggins. One hundred eighty-five copies printed by hand at the Village Press, Hingham, Massachusetts, by Fred & Bertha Goudy, and finished the 19th day of November, 1904.

PAGES: [8] + 19 + [9]. Size 4¾ x 6⅛ inches.

DESIGNS: Five illustrations by Arthur J. Gaskin. Title page and double border by W. A. Dwiggins. Band under half title, 6-line initial 'T,' 4-line initial 'G,' and press mark (second) by F. W. Goudy.

BINDING: Gray paper boards, paper label on back.

1904 EDITION: 185 copies at $1.50 on Arches, 7 on Japan Vellum. Village type. Ransom No. 7.

COMMENT: About a hundred copies were destroyed in the Parker Building fire. The 2-line initials are Cheltenham. The introduction by William Morris was not written especially for this edition, but is copied from an English edition.

Fugitive Items

19. THE HINGHAM SOCIETY OF ARTS AND CRAFTS Established in 1901, OBJECT

Four-page folder, 7 x 9¼ inches. Village type, 7-line initial 'T.' 1500 copies, August. Ransom No. B-2.

20. THE HINGHAM SOCIETY OF ARTS and Crafts announces its third exhibition

Leaf, 6¾ x 3¼, printed one side in black, with circular 4-line insignia of the Society; 7 lines in Village type, August 10.

21. REMOVAL ANNOUNCEMENT

Announcement No. 7. Four-page folder, 4⅝ x 7 inches. Village type. Besides announcing the removal of the Press from Park Ridge, contains lists of books for sale, out of print and in preparation. *Emerson As*

Seer, reported as in press, was set in type and Rudolph Ruzicka had completed wood blocks for a 2-color portrait of Emerson, a few proofs of which still exist. All work on this book, including the original MS., was destroyed in the Parker Building fire. August 20.

1904

22. STATEMENT

Leaf, 5¾ x 4¼, printed one side in black, in Village and black letter type, requesting payment for books.

23. Massachusetts

MASSACHUSETTS | AN OLD AND PROSPEROUS | DEMOCRACY AND A SAFE | SOCIAL ORDER · AN ADDRESS | By CHARLES WILLIAM ELIOT | HINGHAM · MASS | THE VILLAGE PRESS | M·DCCCC·V

1905

COLOPHON: Printed with the author's permission by Fred and Bertha Goudy at The Village Press, Hingham, Massachusetts, in August, 1905. Two hundred fifty copies.

PAGES: [6] + 15 + [7]. Size 4¼ x 5¾ inches.
DESIGNS: Second press mark.
BINDING: Blue paper boards.
EDITION: 250 copies on Vale Press watermarked paper. Village type. Ransom No. 9.
COMMENT: President Eliot, in a letter to Mr. Goudy

1905 giving permission to reprint the address, expressed surprise that anybody would want to pay $1 for such a slight thing.

24. The Lyf of Seynt Kenelme

The Lyf of Seynt Kenelme Kynge | and Martir, from Caxton's Golden | Legend, with a Note on the | Origin of the Text | [*fleuron in red*]

COLOPHON: Thus endeth *The Lyf of Seynt Kenelme, Kynge and Martir,* from Caxton's *Golden Legend,* with drawings taken from *The Quest.* Printed by Fred and Bertha Goudy at The Village Press, Hingham, Massachusetts in August MCMv. 160 copies.

PAGES: [10] + 15 + [7]. Size 5 x 6½ inches.

DESIGNS: Two drawings from *The Quest.*

BINDING: Boards covered with brown paper; pattern designed by F. W. Goudy.

EDITION: 160 copies on Van Gelder Zonen handmade. Introduction in Village, text in American Type Founders' Flemish. Ransom No. 8.

COMMENT: The first book utilizing a type other than Village. *The Quest* was a little magazine hand-printed by the Birmingham (England) Guild of Handicraft, for whom Mr. D. B. Updike was American representative.

25. The Hollow Land — 1905

The | Hollow | Land | [*floral band*] | BY WILLIAM | MORRIS

COLOPHON: Here ends *The Hollow Land, A Tale*, by William Morris. Reprinted from *The Oxford & Cambridge Magazine*. Printed by hand at The Village Press, Hingham, Massachusetts, by Frederic W. & Bertha M. Goudy, from the Village type, and finished this second day of October, 1905. Frontispiece illustration from drawing by Walter J. Enright; illustration on page 43 from drawing by Bror. J. Olsson Nordfeldt; the Note by Cyrus Lauron Hooper; and double border, title and initial by Mr. Goudy, the designer of the fount. Composition by Mrs. Goudy. Two hundred twenty copies. Sold at The Village Press.

PAGES: [6]+67+[7]. Size 6¾ x 8½ inches.

DESIGNS: Frontispiece by Walter J. Enright. Illustration on page 43 by Bror. J. Olsson Nordfeldt. Frontispiece and title page framed in all-around borders; floral bands on pages 5 and 7; 10-line initial 'D' in red and black on page 9 and maple leaf ornament used throughout text, all by F. W. Goudy. Second press mark.

BINDING: Gray paper boards, linen back; title in red on side.

FRONTISPIECE AND TITLE PAGE (ITEM NO. 25)

ILLUSTRATION BY W. J. ENRIGHT · BORDERS, LETTERING AND FLORAL BAND BY F. W. GOUDY

EDITION: 220 copies on Whatman, 200 for sale at $4; after January 15, 1906, $5. Village type. Ransom No. 10.

COMMENT: *The Hollow Land* was the third book begun at The Village Press. The title page section was printed on Thanksgiving Day 1903, at Park Ridge, Ill., but the balance of the book, beginning at page 17, was printed at Hingham, Mass.

The drawing by Nordfeldt was made with a toothpick for pen while he and Robert Bruere were living with the Goudys at Hingham.

Of the 220 copies, only about 85 survived the fire which destroyed the Press on January 10, 1908.

Robert Wiebking, hearing Mr. Goudy say that he wished he had an initial 'L' for page 7, designed, cut and cast this for him. He also cut and cast the maple leaf ornament without charge.

A dummy copy, consisting of three or four printed sections and blank leaves, bound in vellum, was exhibited at the Louisiana Purchase Exposition in St. Louis, 1904.

An inscription in one copy by the author of the prefatory Note reads as follows: "I remember times when Goudy had good reason to be discouraged. But he wasn't. —Cyrus Lauron Hooper."

1905 26. At the Fireside

AT | THE FIRESIDE | John D. Long | [*fleuron*] | Hingham, Massachusetts | THE VILLAGE PRESS | 1905

COLOPHON: *At the Fireside*, written by John D. Long, is printed for him and his friends by Frederic and Bertha Goudy at The Village Press, Hingham, Massachusetts. Finished this twentieth day of November, MCMV. 200 copies.

PAGES: [6]+39+[7]. Size 5⅛ x 8 inches.

DESIGNS: Six-line initial 'A' in red, page 7; leaf and hand-lettered title lines on title page by F. W. Goudy; second press mark.

BINDING: Boards, blue paper, pasted white label in red on side.

EDITION: 200 copies at $2.50 on Arches. Village type. Ransom No. 11.

COMMENT: In 27 copies, 'mystify' on page 33 is mis-spelled 'mistify.' Privately printed for Mr. John D. Long, who allowed the Press to retain enough copies to supply subscribers desiring them.

27. The Gypsy Trail

THE | GYPSY TRAIL [*in red*] | BY | RUDYARD KIPLING | [*spot*] | *BOSTON* | ALFRED BARTLETT

COLOPHON: Printed by Fred and Bertha Goudy at The Village Press, Hingham, Mass. 1905

PAGES: [2]+[12 unnumbered]+[2]. Size 4 x 4¾ inches.

DESIGNS: Frontispiece by E. M. Bird.

BINDING: Gray-green boards, white pasted label on side, printed in red and black.

EDITION: 1000 copies. Caslon No. 471 type.

28. The Gypsy Trail

THE | GYPSY TRAIL [in red] | BY | RUDYARD KIPLING | [spot] | Hingham, Mass. | Fred & Bertha Goudy | 1905

COLOPHON: Printed by Fred & Bertha Goudy at The Village Press, Hingham, Mass., in the month of December 1905. 39 copies.

PAGES: [10]+[12 unnumbered]+[10]. Size 4½ x 5¾ inches.

DESIGNS: Frontispiece by E. M. Bird.

BINDING: Blue boards.

EDITION: 39 copies on Vale Press watermarked paper. Set in Caslon No. 471 type. Ransom No. 12.

COMMENT: Printed for a Christmas gift, using the composition done for Alfred Bartlett (item 27) with altered title page and colophon.

1905

Fugitive Items

29. LIST of the BOOKS FOR SALE & IN PREPARATION
Announcement No. 8. Four-page folder on Van Gelder Zonen, 6⅜ x 9 inches, in black; Village type. Announces as in press *Emerson As Seer*, 230 copies (see No. 21). *The Nonne Preestes Tale*, 140 copies, announced as in preparation, was never begun. January.

30. SUBSCRIPTION BLANK
Leaf, 4⅜ x 6¼, perforated in half and printed one side in black, inviting subscriptions to all publications.

31. THE HINGHAM GLEE CLUB, Fourth Annual Concert
Pamphlet, 12 pages, stitched, 4⅛ x 9 inches. Rectangular scroll work in red on cover.

32. Lent 1905, CHURCH OF ST. JOHN THE EVANGELIST
Four-page folder, 3⅝ x 4⅝ inches. Village and a gothic type; 5-line initial 'A' in red. Ransom No. B-3.

33. Four Poems

1906

FOUR POEMS | THE BALLAD OF THE STRANGER | KING RETRO · THE ROYAL PEDI- | GREE · AND · A DREAM I HAD · BY | JAMES RUSSELL LOWELL | (Now first collected) | HINGHAM | Printed for private distribution | THE VILLAGE PRESS | 1906

1906

COLOPHON: The four poems written by James Russell Lowell and here first collected, are printed and bound by Frederic and Bertha Goudy at The Village Press, in Hingham, Massachusetts, and finished March 10, 1906. Fifty copies only have been printed, for private distribution, and the type distributed. This copy is No.—

PAGES: [4]+32+[4]. Size 5¾ x 9 inches.

BINDING: Blue boards, linen back; title printed in black on side.

EDITION: 50 numbered copies on Arches at $6. Village type. Ransom No. 13.

COMMENT: Done for P. K. Foley of Boston. The last book printed at Hingham. The money received from it ($75) made possible the removal to New York.

Fugitive Item

34. FOUR POEMS BY JAMES RUSSELL LOWELL

Leaf, 5¾ x 9, on Arches, printed in black on one side in Village type. Prospectus offering 50 numbered copies until March 20, 1906, at $6.

DESTRUCTION OF THE PARKER BUILDING
225 FOURTH AVENUE, NEW YORK, N.Y.
THE PRESS OCCUPIED A PART OF THE TWELFTH FLOOR

PUBLICATIONS OF THE VILLAGE PRESS
AT NEW YORK CITY, NEW YORK
1906  1913

35. The Princess of the Tower

THE PRINCESS OF THE TOWER | THE WISE MEN FROM THE EAST | AND · TO THE WINGED VICTORY | BY | BLISS CARMAN | [*fleuron in red*] | New York | THE VILLAGE PRESS | Privately printed | 1906

COLOPHON: Here ends *The Princess of the Tower*, *The Wise Men from the East*, and *To the Winged Victory*, three poems written by Bliss Carman, and now first collected. Sixty-two copies (58 on hand-made paper and 4 on Roman vellum) printed for private distribution by Frederic and Bertha Goudy at The Village Press, New York, December 1906. This is copy No.—

PAGES: [8] + 18 + [8]. Size 6½ x 10⅛ inches.

DESIGNS: Five-line initial 'O' on page 5.

BINDING: Blue boards, linen back; title printed in black on side.

EDITION: 58 numbered copies on Arches, 4 on Roman vellum. Village type. Ransom No. 15.

1906 36. The Perfect Woman

THE | PERFECT WOMAN | AS DESCRIBED IN | THE XXXI CHAP- | TER OF PROVERBS | BEGINNING WITH | THE TENTH | VERSE | [*fleuron*] | 1906 | The Village Press | New York

PAGES: Reported to be 32. Size 3½ x 5⅛ inches.

DESIGNS: Opening page of text specially drawn; printed in red, blue and black, with uncial initials in red or blue.

BINDING: Boards, title printed in red on side.

EDITION: 30 copies on Arches printed for Hedwig and Kendall Banning. Village type. Ranson No. 14.

COMMENT: It had been planned to have the initial letter on the first text page stamped in gold by a bookbinder. A few copies were printed and stamped, but it proved impossible to register the initial exactly and the plan was abandoned. The stamped sheets were destroyed, except for one retained by Mr. Goudy.

A special copy was printed for Dr. Louise Acres, Mrs. Goudy's physician. This contained the following special colophon: *The Perfect Woman*, as described in the Old Testament, is printed and bound for Louise Acres by Fred and Bertha Goudy at The Village Press, New York, Dec. 1906. One copy.

37. Jack and Jill   1906

JACK AND JILL | According to the Modern | School of Fiction | By | W. G. Bowdoin | Author of The Little Girl and her Doll | [*fleuron*] | Privately Printed | Brooklyn·New York | Christmas | M·CM·VI

COLOPHON: Of this edition two hundred copies have been printed at The Village Press and the type distributed. This is No.—

PAGES: [4]+15+[5]. Size 4¾ x 7 inches.

DESIGNS: Frontispiece by Charles P. Schmidt, Jr., 7-line initial 'I' in red, page 5.

BINDING: Blue boards, vellum back, with pasted white label on side, printed in black. Alternative binding: brown paper cover, with title printed on side in black.

EDITION: 200 numbered copies, on Fabriano, privately printed for the author, to be sold by him at $1. Village type.

Fugitive Items

38. NOTICE to...BUYERS OF THE VILLAGE PRESS BOOKS

Announcement No. 9 (not numbered). Four-page folder, 4⅜ x 6¾, announcing the removal of The Village Press from Hingham to New York (12th floor, 225 Fourth Avenue).

1906
FREDERIC AND BERTHA GOUDY · THE VILLAGE PRESS · AN ANNOUNCEMENT OF ITS WORK AND AIMS · TOGETHER WITH A LIST OF ITS PUBLICATIONS

FROM THE FIRST PAGE OF ANNOUNCEMENT NO. 10

(ITEM 39)

39. FREDERIC and BERTHA GOUDY, ANNOUNCEMENT
Announcement No. 10. Sixteen-page folder, sewed, 5½ x 8¼ inches. Contains extended note on the aims of the Press, also complete catalog of books for sale, in press, and in preparation, with numerous illustrations. Issued January.

40. Tommy and Betty — 1907

TOMMY AND BETTY | By | GEORGIA M·LEE | [*fleuron in brown*] | New York | Printed for Private Distribution | THE VILLAGE PRESS | 1907

COLOPHON: Here ends *Tommy and Betty* as written by Georgia M. Lee. Printed and bound for her and her friends, in March, 1907, by Frederic & Bertha Goudy at The Village Press, New York. Composed in Village type: frontispiece illustration by Ruth Mary Hallock. 103 copies printed, and this copy is Number —

PAGES: [10] + 49 + [7]. Size 6½ x 8½ inches.

DESIGNS: Frontispiece by Ruth Mary Hallock, headband by F. W. Goudy.

BINDING: Blue boards, cloth back, title printed in black on side.

EDITION: 103 numbered copies on Fabriano. Village type.

COMMENT: Privately printed for Mrs. Georgia M. Lee. The power press, first used at Hingham, broke down during this job, threatening to make impossible delivery of the copy which Mrs. Lee required for some special occasion. However, the press was repaired and the book successfully completed in March in time for the event.

1907 41. Songs for a Wedding Day

SONGS [in red] | FOR A | WEDDING DAY | A CYCLE OF XXIV POEMS | OF LOVE TRIUMPHANT | EDITED BY | KENDALL | BANNING [last four words in red scroll frame] | New York | THE TRIPTYCH | 1907

COLOPHON: *Songs for a Wedding Day* selected and edited by Kendall Banning. Set in the Village type by Bertha Goudy, arranged and printed for The Triptych at The Village Press, New York, by Frederic and Bertha Goudy in April 1907, in an edition limited to One Hundred Two copies.

PAGES: [10]+[44 unnumbered]+[6]. Size 7¼ x 10¼ inches.

DESIGNS: Frontispiece in photogravure *Love Triumphant*, by G. F. Watts; 6-line initial 'M' and scroll frame on title page, both in red, by F. W. Goudy. Monogram (reproduced on page 57) used as press mark.

BINDING: Brown boards with paper label on back. Some copies with vellum back, title in gold on side.

EDITION: 102 copies in black and red on Arches; copies in boards for sale at $7.50; copies in full limp vellum, $10. Village type. Ransom No. 16.

COMMENT: Arranged and printed for The Triptych, originally J. Chambers, Wm. Jordan and W. M. Stone.

42. Book Plates of Elisha B. Bird   1907

A BOOKLET DEVOTED TO | *The* BOOK PLATES *of* | ELISHA BROWN BIRD | BEING A COLLECTION PRINTED | IN PHOTOGRAVURE [*elaborate full-page design hand-lettered by Bird with monogram 'E.B.'; all in photogravure*

COLOPHON: This edition of *Elisha Brown Bird, His Book Plates*, printed for Winfred Porter Truesdell, Arlington, Massachusetts, consists of one hundred and ten copies on Van Gelder handmade paper, and forty copies on Japan Vellum. The text has been composed by Bertha M. Goudy, in Village type designed by Frederic W. Goudy, and printed by them at The Village Press, New York, in September, 1907. This copy is No.—

PAGES: [6] + [20 text, unnumbered] + [29 plates, unnumbered] + [6]. Size 6 x 9 inches.

DESIGNS: Plates, frontispiece and title page in photogravure; also headband and 13-line initial 'A' in red and black by E. B. Bird.

BINDING: Green boards, vellum back. Design with monogram 'E. B.' on cover in two tones of gold.

EDITION: 110 copies on Van Gelder, 40 on Japan Vellum. Village type.

COMMENT: More book plates are described in the text than are illustrated in the plates.

1907 43. The Lover's Hours

THE LOVER'S HOURS | POEMS | By | FILSON YOUNG | [*circular monogram 'M. K.'*] | New York | Mitchell Kennerley | M | CM | VII

COLOPHON: This edition of *The Lover's Hours* written by Filson Young, has been arranged and printed for Mitchell Kennerley by Fred and Bertha Goudy at The Village Press, New York, in November, 1907. One hundred fifty copies printed, and this is copy No.—

PAGES: [8]+16+[8]. Size 5¾ x 8½ inches.

DESIGNS: Monogram 'M.K.' in circle on title page.

BINDING: Edition destroyed before binding.

EDITION: 150 numbered copies on Kelmscott Hammer and Anvil. Village type.

COMMENT: The printed sheets were being held at the Press pending selection of a binder. Two sets had, however, been sent to the Library of Congress to secure copyright. One additional set had been delivered to Mr. Kennerley the day before the Parker Building fire and sent by him to the hotel of Mr. John Lane, who was to be the English publisher. After the fire Mr. Kennerley learned that Mr. Lane had left before receiving the sheets, which were recovered from the hotel, bound, and now constitute the only other extant

copy of this book. This is now in the F. W. Goudy 1907
Collection in the Vassar College Library, Poughkeepsie, N.Y. All other sheets were destroyed in the fire, together with the equipment of The Village Press.

44. There is no Unbelief

THERE | IS NO UNBELIEF | A POEM | By | Elizabeth York Case | [*fleuron in black*] | NEW YORK | IVAN SOMERVILLE & COMPANY | PUBLISHERS

COLOPHON: [*On copyright page*] Designed and printed at The Village Press, New York.

PAGES: [8] + [22 *unnumbered*] + [4]. Size 5¼ x 6¼ inches.

DESIGNS: Double page border decoration in olive; title hand-lettered; 6-line initial 'T,' all by F. W. Goudy.

BINDING: Paper-covered boards. Hand-lettered title in red and olive decoration on side by F. W. Goudy.

EDITION: About 1,000 copies on Old Stratford. For sale at $1. Set in Old Style Antique. Ransom No. 17.

COMMENT: The first of three books composed and printed under the style of Ivan Somerville & Co., publishers. Mr. Goudy, who was to do the printing, and Mr. Somerville, who was to do the selling, constituted the firm.

1907 45. Faith and Reason

FAITH AND REASON [in red] | A POEM BY | Elizabeth York Case | [fleuron in red] | NEW YORK | IVAN SOMERVILLE & COMPANY | PUBLISHERS

COLOPHON: [On copyright page] Designed and printed at The Village Press, New York.

PAGES: [6] + [16 unnumbered] + [6]. Size 5¼ x 6¼ inches.

DESIGNS: Double page border decoration in red; title hand-lettered; 5-line initial 'T' by F. W. Goudy.

BINDING: Paper-covered boards. Hand-lettered title and decoration in red on side by F. W. Goudy.

EDITION: About 1,000 copies on Old Stratford. For sale at $1. Composed in Old Style Antique.

COMMENT: The second of three books composed and printed under the style of Ivan Somerville & Co., publishers.

46. A Christmas Carol

A | CHRISTMAS CAROL | By SIR NOEL PATON | [square unit] | NEW YORK, | IVAN SOMERVILLE & COMPANY | PUBLISHERS

COLOPHON: [On copyright page] Designed and printed at The Village Press, New York.

PAGES: [6] + [16 unnumbered] + [6]. Size 5¼ x 6¼ inches.

DESIGNS: Double page border decoration in olive and title hand-lettered by F. W. Goudy.

BINDING: Paper-covered boards. Hand-lettering in red and decoration in green on side by F. W. Goudy.

EDITION: About 1,000 copies on Old Stratford. For sale at $1. Set in Old Style Antique.

COMMENT: The last of three books composed and printed under the style of Ivan Somerville & Co., publishers.

47. The Gate of Peace

THE | GATE OF PEACE [in red] | A POEM | by BLISS CARMAN | [fleuron in red] | NEW YORK: | THE VILLAGE PRESS | 1907

COLOPHON: One hundred twelve copies of *The Gate of Peace* printed by Frederic and Bertha Goudy at The Village Press, New York, in December, 1907. This copy is No.—

PAGES: [8] + [17 unnumbered] + [7]. Size 6½ x 10¼ inches.

DESIGNS: Six-line initial 'A' in red; leaf in black on last text page by F. W. Goudy.

1907 BINDING: Blue boards, cloth back. Title in black on side.

EDITION: 112 numbered copies, signed by the author, on Kelmscott Hammer and Anvil. Set in Original Old Style Italic and Caslon No. 471. Ransom No. 18.

COMMENT: The only copies saved from the Parker Building fire were 19 which had been delivered to Bliss Carman and 5 which had been mailed to purchasers by Mr. Goudy.

Fugitive Items

48. EXTRACTS FROM THE BOOK BEAUTIFUL

Broadside, printed on Kelmscott Hammer and Anvil, 11¾ x 17¼ inches, containing quotation from T. J. Cobden-Sanderson. 13-line initial 'T' in red by F. W. Goudy. 160 copies in Village type, for sale at 35 cents. About half destroyed in Parker Building fire. July. Ransom No. B-4.

49. BOOKS FOR SALE AND IN PREPARATION

Announcement No. 11 (not numbered). Leaf 7¼ x 11 inches, printed both sides in black, listing as completed and for sale *Songs for a Wedding Day, The Book Beatiful—Extracts;* and as in preparation *Songs and Verses, Forefathers' Day* and *The Sermon on the Mount.*

50. IN MEMORIAM SARAH EMILY CONDIT   1907

Pamphlet, 20 pages self cover, 6¾ x 9¼ inches, privately printed in Village type on Vale Press watermarked paper. Contains a portrait of Mrs. Condit in photogravure; 7-line initial 'O' by F. W. Goudy. 145 copies. October.

51. THE NEXT MEETING OF THE STOWAWAYS

Leaf, 6¾ x 9⅜ inches, printed one side in black in Original Old Style Italic, with headband of ship and sun. November.

52. THE BUNCH OF VIOLETS

Pamphlet, 24 pages 4¾ x 7¼ inches, Japanese gray paper cover. Privately printed for the author, W. G. Bowdoin, in Village type on Kelmscott Hammer and Anvil with frontispiece in photogravure from a study by Agnes Vinton Luther. Triangular decorative spot and 7-line initial 'T,' both in red, by F. W. Goudy. Press monogram in colophon. 102 numbered copies for sale by the author at $1. November.

53. INTERIOR DECORATION

A monthly magazine edited by J. M. Bowles, 16 pages, 9½ x 12¼ inches, paper cover. Design, hand-

1907 lettering and decorative initials by F. W. Goudy. Set in Village type by Bertha Goudy. December.

Contains full-page advertisement of The Village Press (only payment received for this job), announcing as in press for immediate publication *The Sermon on the Mount; The Gate of Peace* by Bliss Carman; *Forefathers' Day* by James Russell Lowell; and *Songs and Verses* by Edmund Waller.

54. THE GUILD OF BOOK-WORKERS

Pamphlet, 28 pages 5 x 8 inches, stiff blue paper cover; 7-line initial 'T' by F. W. Goudy.

55. CITY & COUNTRY HOMES

Advertising booklet, 12 pages 10 x 14⅞ inches. Decorative spot in yellow on cover and page 10, also 8-line initial 'I' on page 3 by F. W. Goudy. Done for Hoggson Bros.

56. NOTES ON LETTER DESIGN

An article by F. W. Goudy which appeared in the magazine *Graphic Arts*, edited by Henry Lewis Johnson (pages 361 to 368). Headband and 6-line initial 'T,' 4-line initial 'O,' 5-line initial 'C,' and 3-line initial 'T' by F. W. Goudy.

The first page, No. 361, was set in Kennerley at The Village Press; includes reproduction of title page of catalog issued by the New York Metropolitan Museum of Art on the occasion of the Hudson-Fulton Celebration in the fall of 1909, together with text page from this catalog in Village type and other specimens. 1907

57. THE GATE OF PEACE, A POEM

Four-page folder, 6 x 10⅝ inches, 7-line initial 'A' by F. W. Goudy. Prospectus offering 65 of 112 copies for sale at $5; price after Feb. 1, 1908 to be $7.50. Offers also 3 special copies of *The Princess of the Tower*.

The Destruction of The Village Press by Fire

[AS TOLD BY FREDERIC W. GOUDY]

On the evening of January 10, 1908, occurred one of the greatest misfortunes of my life, the complete loss by fire of The Village Press equipment, books completed and in the making, drawings, blocks, work books, tools—everything. The Village Press at this time occupied a large room on the 12th floor of the Parker Building at 19th Street and Fourth Avenue. 1908

Except for a happy circumstance only, it is possible that we—Bertha, my son and myself—might have

1908 been added also to the list of those who lost their lives in that conflagration, since for weeks past, excepting on that particular Friday night, we had worked every evening until the elevator stopped running. In the late afternoon an old Chicago friend of ours, Eva Dean, now of Los Angeles, came in and asked Bertha to go shopping with her. As there seemed nothing especially important to keep her—we had just finished the binding of Bliss Carman's *Gate of Peace*—I, of course, was glad to have her go, and said I would take Frederic and go home early myself; we were living on 117th Street near Morningside Park.

About eight-thirty, as I remember, I was hugging the radiator, reading. Bertha probably was sewing when the telephone rang. Bertha took down the receiver and turning to me said, "It's Everett Currier," and speaking into the phone said "Is the Parker Building on fire?" Evidently Currier asked if I were there, because she again said, "Yes, is the Parker Building burning?" Then she turned to me and said, "Currier says the Parker Building is on fire and you'd better hurry down." In a few minutes I was on the subway. Emerging at 19th Street I found myself within the fire lines and was promptly ejected by the police, as there already was danger of falling bricks, burning brands, etc. They didn't even want me to go to my own fire. I watched the blazing building from a nearby corner until I saw our floor, the 12th, where our shop was located, go down. Hunting a telephone I called Bertha and told her "the joke is on us, everything is gone." I presume that night we did sleep—some. The next day I went down again. Fearing danger of falling walls, as the building was completely gutted from the 5th floor up to the 12th, the city authorities had piled timbers over Fourth Avenue in front of the building so that, in case of collapse, the masonry would not crash through into the subway. The walls, however, were intact and I believe have since been used without much additional work on them, while rebuilding the interior. The building, now known as the Pocono, still stands, but I have never since entered it.

A few days after the fire, when things had cooled down, I was in the neighborhood again and it seemed to me that a portion of the 12th floor, the southeastern corner, had not entirely gone down. Suddenly I remembered that a few months before I had, for some reason or other, had occasion to look at the matrices of the Village type which I kept carelessly in a pigeon-

1908 hole of my desk. While I was looking at them my friend, Oscar Shaw, Superintendent or Manager of the Parker Building, who frequently dropped in for a few minute's chat while we worked, (his office was also on the 12th floor) came in and, catching sight of the rows of matrices as they lay on my desk, asked what they were. I told him and he expressed surprise that I kept them so carelessly unprotected. He said "they probably are valuable." My reply was that they could, of course, be replaced, as the original patterns were in Chicago at the shop of Mr. Robert Wiebking who engraved them for me, but only at some considerable expense. He said, "why don't you let me put them in the safe in my office?" And he did. So on the visit to the building referred to above I remembered the incident and it occurred to me that possibly the safe had not dropped. I got in touch with Mr. Shaw, who lived in Brooklyn, and he said that the safe had not gone down, being near an outside wall, and as soon as it could be opened, he would get the package of matrices for me. He was certain they would be found undamaged and intact, and sure enough, such was the case—the only item of our entire equipment that I ever saw again. Afterwards they were sold to a New York publisher.

A Bibliography of The Village Press

Our workshop adjoined the laboratory of Dr. Lee de Forest, who at that time was working on his wireless telephone, and I frequently could hear his voice patiently repeating "Hello! hello!—do you hear me now?" as he spoke into his microphone, the receiver, I believe, being in the Metropolitan Insurance Tower. Across the hall was an engraving establishment and on this particular evening a night force was at work. When the alarm was given, their exit by the stairs was cut off and several men took refuge on the roof of the building, from which finally they were able to reach the roof of the old Florence Hotel adjoining the Parker Building and several stories lower, by means of ropes. If our friend had not come in as she did, we probably would have remained later, as usual, and have been trapped as they were. Several firemen unfortunately perished. Peace to their ashes.

There was no insurance; times were hard, money was scarce and the building was "fireproof" as indeed it was, for no fire escaped into any other building; it was all ours. The blow was a heavy one, but it developed certain pleasing facts, that several whom I regarded merely as business friends proved to be warm friends in time of need and were quick to offer aid.

1908

1908 The volumes given under 1908 were in various stages of manufacture at the time of the fire. Though never completed, they are here listed, as fragments of some items have survived.

58. The Sermon in the Mount

THE SERMON IN THE MOUNT | BEING CHAPTERS V, VI AND VII OF THE GOSPEL | ACCORDING TO SAINT MATTHEW

COLOPHON: Never written.

PAGES: Size 9¼ x 12½ inches.

DESIGNS: Numerous initials and 4 all-around page borders and reverses by F. W. Goudy. Nine full-page drawings by R. Anning Bell of Liverpool loaned by Alfred Bartlett of Boston.

EDITION: 160 copies projected in black and red on Kelmscott Hammer and Anvil. Village type.

COMMENT: A considerable portion of this book was in type, but all work was completely destroyed before its completion in the Parker Building fire. Fortunately a single page (reduced) is reproduced in Barnard's *Monograph on F. W. Goudy* (see 1912), while a double page of the actual composition was used in the magazine *Interior Decoration* (Item No. 53).

Each of the 4 double page borders had meant 6 or

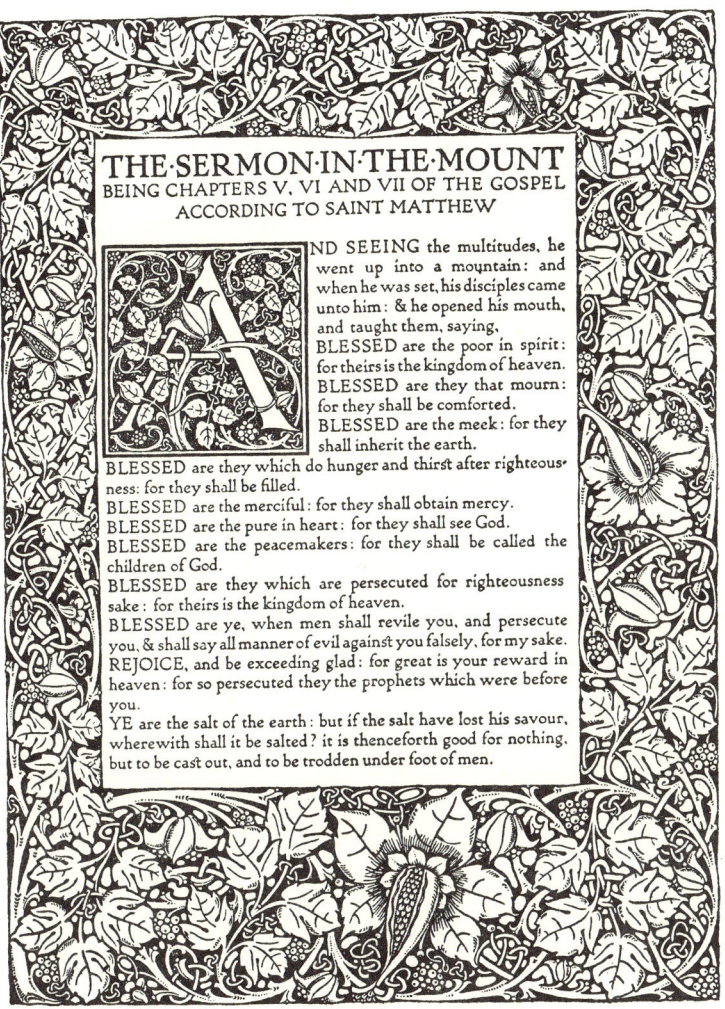

THE SERMON IN THE MOUNT

(ITEM NO. 58)

1908 8 evening's labor drawing. The illustrations by R. A. Bell had already been used as a series of 12 in a calendar. By great good fortune these originals had been returned to Boston only a few days prior to the fire.

59. Forefathers' Day

FOREFATHERS' DAY, An Address by James Russell Lowell delivered at Plymouth, Mass., December 21, 1885

Colophon: Never written.

Pages: Size 5 x 7½ inches.

Designs: It was to contain a portrait of Mr. Lowell in photogravure.

Edition: 85 copies projected in black and red on Kelmscott Hammer and Anvil. Village type.

Comment: The printed sheets, which were almost completed, together with the unfinished forms were destroyed in the Parker Building fire. Mr. Goudy recalls that the sheets he did complete for this book were the best examples of hand-presswork he has ever done.

60. Emerson as Seer

Emerson as Seer, An Address by Dr. Charles Eliot

Comment: For this book Rudolph Ruzicka cut on wood a 2-color portrait of Emerson, of which a very few impressions are extant, although the blocks themselves were subsequently destroyed by the artist. All work on the book was lost in the Parker Building fire. **1908**

61. Simeon Solomon

SIMEON SOLOMON | AN APPRECIATION BY | JULIA ELLSWORTH FORD | [*decorative head in sepia*] | NEW YORK | FREDERIC FAIRCHILD SHERMAN | MCMVIII

COMMENT: Work on this volume, which was to have been published by Scribners, was well advanced, 5 reams having been printed, when it was completely destroyed in the Parker Building fire.

Another edition, with the original title page which had been designed and hand-lettered by Mr. Goudy for The Village Press issue, was published later in 1908 by F. F. Sherman.

Fugitive Items

62. ANNOUNCEMENT OF IVAN SOMERVILLE & CO. **1907**

Eight-page folder, 5⅞ x 9¾ inches. List of Fall publications, including as in preparation *Our Alphabet, A Handbook of Letters*, the earliest reference to *The Alphabet*, actually published in 1918. Monogram 'I. S. & Co.' and 4-line initial 'I' by F. W. Goudy.

1908 63. ADVERTISEMENT OF THE VILLAGE PRESS

Full-page advertisement, 9 x 12 inches, for *Interior Decoration*. Heading "The Village Press" hand-lettered in gothic style. Announced as ready *Songs for a Wedding Day* (Item No. 41), with others in preparation. A paragraph under heading solicits job and book work.

The First Work Following the Fire

Following the complete destruction of The Village Press and its equipment on January 10, 1908, Mr. and Mrs. Goudy occupied an apartment at 28th Street and Clarendon Road in Flatbush. No Village Press work was done here, but after their removal to 6th Avenue and 7th Street, also in Brooklyn, a supply of Kennerley and Forum type was received from Wiebking and a small stand of cases made composition again possible. It was here that Mrs. Goudy set one of the rarest Village Press-Bruce Rogers items, the first work of the Press since the fire, *Mr. Walpole's Friends in Boston*, (item No. 64) from copy which Mr. Rogers had in his pocket when he came to a mid-day dinner one Sunday. The first page, composed during the afternoon and proved, showed not a single error.

From the Spring of 1912 Mr. Goudy supplemented

the type-setting at his apartment by a growing equipment at his office, 132 Madison Avenue, New York. It was here that most of the work done in 1912 and 1913 was produced.

64. MR. WALPOLE'S FRIENDS IN BOSTON   1910

Pamphlet, 28 pages, 5¾ x 9 inches, bound in blue wrappers. Set in Original Old Style Italic by Bertha Goudy, with decorations by Bruce Rogers; 27 copies privately printed by Mr. Rogers for the Walpole Society at the Riverside Press, Cambridge, Mass.

65. Songs and Verses   1911

SONGS AND | VERSES | SELECTED FROM THE WORKS | of | Edmund Waller, Esq. | NEW YORK | The Village Press | 1911

COLOPHON: One hundred ten copies of this booklet have been printed at The Village Press by Frederic and Bertha Goudy in March, 1911, and is the first issue from the Press since its total destruction by fire January 10, 1908.

PAGES: [2] + 19 + [3]. Size 6 x 9¼ inches.

BINDING: Blue boards, title in black on side.

EDITION: 110 copies on Glaslan, none for sale. Original Old Style Italic and Caslon No. 471. Ransom No. 19.

1911 COMMENT: For this volume, the first issue of The Village Press since the fire in January, 1908, Mr. Goudy designed a new press mark similar to the third (reproduced on page 57) but with the addition of a phoenix rising from the ashes. However, it was not used here.

The presswork on this book was done on a little 9 x 12 Golding, now used by the Maverick Press.

THE FOURTH PRESS MARK AND SECOND MONOGRAM
OF THE VILLAGE PRESS

66. A Painter's Holiday

A | PAINTER'S HOLIDAY | and Other Poems | BY | BLISS CARMAN | [*twin hippocampi*] | NEW YORK | PRIVATELY PRINTED | 1911

COLOPHON: One hundred and fifty copies of this book on French hand-made paper privately printed by Frederic Fairchild Sherman.

PAGES: 56. Size 7¼ x 10¼ inches.

DESIGNS: First 3 lines of title page hand lettered by F. W. Goudy.

BINDING: Blue boards, vellum back; title printed on back. **1911**

EDITION: 150 copies on a specially watermarked French paper. Some sheets were printed on parchment, but may never have been bound. Sherman type.

COMMENT: Mr. Goudy had intended to print this book himself on the little Golding press, but found it rather more of an undertaking than he anticipated. The presswork was, therefore, done by N. T. A. Munder, Mr. Goudy printing only 2 style pages for position and impression.

The Sherman type, a special face designed by Mr. Goudy, was first used on this book. It is the most closely fitted ever designed by Mr. Goudy.

67. Verses, by McVickar

VERSES | By | HENRY GOELET McVICKAR | [*five lines of verse*] | *New York* | PRIVATELY PRINTED | 1911

COLOPHON: Fifty-four copies of *Verses* by Henry Goelet McVickar have been printed in June 1911, by Frederic & Bertha Goudy at The Village Press, New York.

PAGES: [6] + 51 + [7]. Size 5½ x 8¼ inches.

DESIGNS: Four-line initial 'J' by F. W. Goudy.

BINDING: Dark blue boards, printed label on back.

1911   EDITION: 54 copies on Glaslan. Kennerley type.

COMMENT: Printed on the small Golding press at 6th Avenue and 7th Street, Brooklyn.

68. Address to the Graduating Class

ADDRESS | TO THE GRADUATING CLASS | MCMXI· OF THE UNITRINIAN | SCHOOL OF PERSONAL | HARMONIZING | FOUNDED BY MARY PERRY KING | AT MOONSHINE, TWILIGHT PARK | IN THE CAT-SKILLS | By | BLISS CARMAN | NEW YORK | *Privately Printed* | 1911

COLOPHON: Two hundred and fifty copies of this address have been printed for the Author under the direction of Frederic W. Goudy, at The Tabard Press, New York, October, 1911.

PAGES: [8] + 27 + [9]. Size 6½ x 10¼ inches.

DESIGNS: Six-line initial 'I' by F. W. Goudy.

BINDING: Blue boards, cloth back, title in black on side.

EDITION: 250 copies on Tuscany. Kennerley and Forum types.

COMMENT: Set by Bertha Goudy; printed at The Tabard Press, New York, in October. Mr. Carman later gave Mr. Goudy an unpublished poem called *If I Were Pan* in payment for his work on this book.

69. Heinrich Heine   1911

HEINRICH HEINE | by | MICHAEL MONAHAN | [spot] | New York and London | Mitchell Kennerley | 1911

COLOPHON: [On copyright page] Composition by The Village Press; presswork by O. H. La Barre.

PAGES: [8] + 47 + [9]. Size 5½ x 8 inches.

DESIGNS: Six-line initial 'H' by F. W. Goudy.

BINDING: Brown boards, title stamped in gold on side.

EDITION: 500 copies on Glaslan. Kennerley and Forum types.

COMMENT: Set by Bertha Goudy; printed by O. H. La Barre, New York.

70. The Door in the Wall

THE DOOR | IN THE WALL | *And Other Stories* | BY | H·G·WELLS | ILLUSTRATED | WITH PHOTOGRAVURES FROM | PHOTOGRAPHS BY | ALVIN LANGDON COBURN | [*decorative monogram 'M.R.' in red*] | NEW YORK & LONDON | MITCHELL KENNERLEY | MCMXI

COLOPHON: This book has been set by Bertha S. Goudy at The Village Press, New York, with types and decorations designed by Frederic W. Goudy, under whose supervision it has been printed by Norman T.

1911 A. Munder & Company, Baltimore, U. S. A. Six hundred copies printed on French hand-made paper, in November, 1911, and the types distributed.

PAGES: [8] + 153 + [7]. Size 11 x 14½ inches.

DESIGNS: Monogram on title page in red, headband and 9-line initial 'O,' 7-line initials 'I,' 'S,' and 2 'T''s in black, 5 hand-lettered lines on title page; all by F. W. Goudy.

BINDING: Magenta boards, cloth back, title in gold on side; paper label on back.

EDITION: 600 copies on a specially made Glaslan, for sale at $7.50. Kennerley type.

COMMENT: It was originally intended to use 18 pt. Caslon for this book, but trial pages seemed too open. Mr. Goudy thereupon designed a new face which he called Kennerley after the publisher, sent the drawings to be cut by Wiebking in Chicago, and within 30 days had the finished type. This was the 16 pt., the first size cut, and was set 36 ems wide instead of 38 as originally planned. The type was set by Mrs. Goudy and the pages shipped to N. T. A. Munder, Baltimore, for printing.

The 10 illustrations were printed in London, but in shipment a nail was driven through 300 of one sub-

THE DOOR IN THE WALL

And Other Stories

BY

H·G·WELLS

ILLUSTRATED
WITH PHOTOGRAVURES FROM
PHOTOGRAPHS BY

ALVIN LANGDON COBURN

NEW YORK & LONDON
MITCHELL KENNERLEY
MCMXI

1911 ject, leaving only 300 complete sets from which that number of perfect books were manufactured. Subsequently the 300 remaining books, lacking one illustration, were bound in light brown boards, with the missing photogravure replaced by an aquatone.

On page 150, 7th line, the letter 'f' is missing from the word 'beautiful.'

Fugitive Items

71. ITALIAN HAND-MADE PAPER

Four-page folder, 9½ x 12¾ inches, in orange and black. Border design by F. W. Goudy. Set by Bertha Goudy; printed by N. T. A. Munder, Baltimore. June.

72. PROSPECTUS FOR *THE DOOR IN THE WALL*

Four-page folder, 11 x 14⅝ inches, in orange and black. Kennerley type. Shows title and text pages, also frontispiece printed from a 400-line screen halftone tipped on. Set by Bertha Goudy and printed by N. T. A. Munder, Baltimore.

73. TYPOGRAPHICA NO. 1

First announcement of the Village Letter Foundery. Pamphlet, 12 pages, 5½ x 8⅜ inches, in black and red on Glaslan, brown paper cover. Shows 14 and 18

pt. Forum, 12, 16 and 18 pt. Kennerley; 4- and 8-line 1911
initial 'T''s by F. W. Goudy. First use (printed in red
on cover) of the revised Press monogram showing a
phoenix rising from the ashes (see page 100).

Set by Bertha Goudy, and 250 copies printed by
N.T. A. Munder, Baltimore. September.

74. DIPLOMA OF THE UNITRINIAN SCHOOL

Leaf, 9⅞ x 13⅜, printed one side in orange-red and
black. Forum type. Architectural framework by F.W.
Goudy. Set by Bertha Goudy; printed elsewhere.

75. PROSPECTUS FOR *BARNARD'S MONOGRAPHS*

Four-page folder, 6 x 9¼ inches; 7-line initial 'A'
by F. W. Goudy. A prospectus of the monograph on
F. W. Goudy that appeared in 1912. At this time Mr.
Goudy was sharing office space with Mr. Barnard at
132 Madison Avenue. Ransom No. B-6. November.

76. THE FIRST CHRISTMAS TREE

Pamphlet, 20 pages 4¼ x 6 inches; gray Ingres (a few
in Japan Vellum) paper cover; 7-line initial 'I' by F.W.
Goudy. Kennerley type; 250 copies privately printed
for Edwin S. Gorham on Arches. Set by Bertha Goudy
and printed by N.T.A. Munder, Baltimore. December.

1912 77. Songs of the Love Unending

SONGS | OF | THE LOVE UNENDING | A SONNET SEQUENCE | by | Kendall Banning | [*circular ornament in red*] | Chicago | Brothers of the Book | 1912

COLOPHON: Three hundred seventy-five copies of *Songs of the Love Unending*, written by Kendall Banning, have been printed for the Brothers of the Book by Frederic and Bertha Goudy at The Village Press, in New York, and finished December 9th, 1912.

The frontispiece is a photogravure reproduction of the painting *Love and Life* by George Frederick Watts.

PAGES: [6]+14+[4]. Size 6¾ x 10 inches.

DESIGNS: Frontispiece in photogravure from the painting *Love and Life* by George F. Watts. Pegasus in red on title page; 8-line initial 'M' by F. W. Goudy. First use in a book of fifth Village Press mark.

BINDING: Blue boards, cloth back; title in black on side.

EDITION: 375 copies on Kelmscott Crown and Sceptre. Goudy Oldstyle type, now called Goudy Lanston. Ransom No. 20.

COMMENT: Printed at 132 Madison Avenue for the Brothers of the Book. The first page is shown under *Page Designs from Modern American Books* in the article

Books: *The Art of the Book* in the *Encyclopedia Britannica*, **1912**
14th edition.

THE FIFTH MARK OF THE VILLAGE PRESS
(*Based on that of John de Colonia, which first appeared in 1481*)

78. New-Year Civilities

NEW-YEAR CIVILITIES | *Being an excerpt from* | SALMA-GUNDI | By | Washington Irving | NEW YORK | PRIVATELY PRINTED | CHRISTMAS | 1912

Colophon: Of this book two hundred copies have been printed for Thomas Nast Fairbanks at The Village Press, in December, 1912.

Pages: [6]+13+[5]. Size 5 x 7½ inches.
Designs: Headband, 6-line initial 'I' by F.W.Goudy.
Binding: Blue boards, title in black on side.

1912 EDITION: 200 copies privately printed on Barcelona paper. Kennerley type.
COMMENT: Done at 132 Madison Avenue.

Fugitive Items

79. AN ARGUMENT FOR... A NATIONAL WEEKLY

Eight-page folder, and cover, 6½ x 8¾ inches. Set by Bertha Goudy in Kennerley and Forum; 50 copies printed for J. O'Hara Cosgrave by the Tabard Press.

80. THE STOWAWAYS

Four-page folder, 6 x 9¾ inches, printed first page only. Invitation to dinner and the theatre, April 30. Done at 132 Madison Avenue.

81. BOOKS NOT DEAD THINGS

Four-page folder, 8½ x 11¾ inches, on Kelmscott Hammer and Anvil, exhibiting "the first impression of the Goudy type." Set in 14 pt. Goudy Oldstyle, subsequently renamed Goudy Antique; now known as Goudy Lanston. Contains a passage from Milton's *Areopagitica: A Speech for the Liberty of Unlicensed Printing*.

The first book use of this type was in *Songs of the Love Unending* (item No. 77). Done at 6th Avenue and 7th Street, Brooklyn; 87 copies, May. Ransom No. B-8.

82. TYPOGRAPHICA NO. 2   1912

Pamphlet, 16 pages 8 x 11¼ inches, self cover; in black and red on Old Stratford. First use (in red on cover) of fifth press mark, based on that of John de Colonia, 1481. The similar mark of Ottaviano Scotto, Venice, 1483, is shown on the back cover. Done at 132 Madison Avenue. June. Ransom No. B-9.

83. BARNARD'S MONOGRAPHS ON DESIGN
    The Work of Frederic W. Goudy, Printer and Craftsman, by Temple Scott

Pamphlet, 28 pages 7½ x 10½ inches, gray Florentine cover; printed in black on Old Stratford. Frontispiece in photogravure of Mr. Goudy from photograph by C. H. Barnard. Headband, cover design, 8-line initial 'S' and 9-line initial 'E' by F. W. Goudy. Fifth press mark. Set in Kennerley by Bertha Goudy. For sale at 50 cents. Done at 132 Madison Avenue. July.

84. AN EXHIBITION

Poster, 14 x 20½ inches, designed and lettered by F. W. Goudy. Announcement of exhibition of photographic art, Montross Art Galleries, Oct. 10-31. Printed in blue-black on coarse brownish-gray paper by F. W. and Bertha Goudy on the hand press at 132 Madison

1912 Avenue. Three outline cameras at top drawn and colored by Max Weber. This was the first annual exhibition of the Pictorial Photographers of America. Less than two dozen printed. October.

85. A DINNER OF THE STOWAWAYS...

Four-page folder, 5⅞ x 7⅝ inches, printed first page only on Italian hand-made; 12-line initial 'A' in gold bronze by F. W. Goudy. Kennerley type. Done at 132 Madison Avenue. October.

86. INTERPRETATIVE PHOTOGRAPHY

Four-page folder, 7½ x 10¼ inches, on Kelmscott Crown and Sceptre. Announcement by Charles H. Barnard in 20 lines of Forum. Photogravure portrait of lady. Done at 132 Madison Avenue. Ransom No. B-5.

87. Good Bishop Valentine

1913 GOOD | BISHOP VALENTINE | *A Prose Fancy* | *By* | RICHARD LE GALLIENNE | PRIVATELY PRINTED | FOR BELLE DA COSTA GREENE | FEBRUARY 13-14 | MCMXIII

PAGES: [6] + 10 + [4]. Size 5 x 7½ inches.
DESIGNS: Seven-line initial 'T' by F. W. Goudy.
BINDING: Boards covered with green wood veneer; label on side with name of recipient in red.

EDITION: 22 copies privately printed on Kelmscott Crown and Sceptre. Kennerley type.

COMMENT: This book was prepared for presentation to the guests at a dinner, and was completed in two days at 132 Madison Avenue.

Fugitive Items

88. THE LITTLE BOOK SHOP AROUND THE CORNER

Four-page folder, 5⅝ x 7⅞ inches, in Forum and Kennerley. Invitation to an exhibition of book bindings by Edith Diehl. Set at 132 Madison Avenue, and printed elsewhere. April.

89. EXHIBITION OF OLD MASTERS

Four-page folder, 7¼ x 10 inches, in red and black, announcing a loan exhibition in aid of the Dickens Centenary Fund. Kennerley and Forum types. Done at 132 Madison Avenue. April 10.

90. PIANOLA RECITAL SEASON

Sixteen-page booklet, 7¾ x 11¼ inches; French fold cover of heavy ivory laid stock, printed in black and red within blind embossed panel. Inside printed in black and red on Old Stratford wove. Decorative de-

1913 signs in red, hand-lettering in black on cover and title page; 9-line initial 'S,' 4-line initial 'A' and headbands by F. W. Goudy. Kennerley and Forum. Set by Bertha Goudy at 132 Madison Avenue; printed elsewhere.

DECORATION FROM TITLE PAGE OF "PIANOLA RECITAL SEASON"
(ITEM NO. 90)

91. S. G. ROSENBAUM, AN APPRECIATION

Booklet, about 24 pages, 12 x 16 inches. Presentation copy on the twenty-fifth anniversary of the founding of the National Cloak & Suit Co. Architectural title page by F. W. Goudy, followed by signatures set in Forum. One copy on vellum, bound in full Russian, gold tooled. October 27.

92. THE FOREST TREES, CHRISTMAS MCMXIII   **1913**
   Eight-page pamphlet, self cover, 8½ x 11¾ inches, printed in red and black in Goudy Antique on Kelmscott Hammer and Anvil. Frontispiece, line plate, *The Forest Trees*, by Earl Horter; 11-line initial 'M' in red by F.W. Goudy. Privately printed for the author, Edward Hungerford, at 132 Madison Avenue. Ransom No. 21. December.

THE PRESS OCCUPIED THE GROUND FLOOR ROOM TO THE RIGHT OF THE FRONT DOOR
DEEPDENE ROAD, FOREST HILLS GARDENS, NEW YORK

PUBLICATIONS OF THE VILLAGE PRESS
AT FOREST HILLS GARDENS, N.Y.
1913  1923

93. THE FIRST GOUDY CHRISTMAS CARD

Leaf, 6¼ x 9 inches, printed one side only in Forum. Large initial 'G'; from a woodcut done in 1571 for a projected missal by Plantin of Antwerp, later used in No. 3 of *Ars Typographica*, page 30, 1920. December.

94. NINE POEMS—WILLIAM BUTLER YEATS **1914**

Pamphlet, 32 pages, 5 x 7½ inches, in blue paper cover; printed in Kennerley and Forum on Kelmscott Crown and Sceptre. Frontispiece original photograph of Yeats by Arnold Genthe. Set by Bertha Goudy and printed by Publishers Printing Co.

Privately printed through Mitchell Kennerley for John Quinn, who used these booklets as place cards at a farewell dinner to Mr. Yeats on April 1. A reprinting containing a few corrections was made immediately after the dinner, so that Mr. Yeats might take a few copies to London. Edition approximately 30.

1914 95. *THE PRINTING ART* at the NATIONAL EXPOSITION
Leaf, 9¼ x 11¾ inches, in Forum with 7-line initial 'E' in red by F. W. Goudy. An invitation to visit the National Printing and Advertising Exposition, New York, April 18-25.

96. A NOVEL TYPE FOUNDERY
Sixteen-page pamphlet, brown paper cover, 5 x 8½ inches, on Old Stratford. Shows types and borders for sale by The Village Press and Letter Foundery. Headband, caduceus and various ornaments and initial letters by F. W. Goudy, besides the types and borders. Set by Bertha Goudy; printed by Rogers & Company, New York.

Prepared for distribution at the National Printing and Advertising Exposition, Grand Central Palace, New York, April 18-25.

CADUCEUS BY F. W. GOUDY, FROM "A NOVEL TYPE FOUNDERY"
(ITEM NO. 96)

97. A NOVEL TYPE FOUNDERY — 1914

Twenty-page pamphlet, self cover, 4¾ x 8⅜ inches, on Old Stratford, showing types and borders included in the preceding item. Also certain sizes subsequently received, namely: the 10, 24, 30, 36, 48 pt. Forum; the 10, 24, 30, 36 pt. Kennerley; and the 18 pt. Kennerley italic. The first 6 and last 7 pages of both items are the same.

98. AMERICAN INSTITUTE OF GRAPHIC ARTS

Four-page folder, 8 x 10¼ inches, on Fabriano; 8-line initial 'A' in red by F. W. Goudy. Prospectus, the first piece of printed matter issued by the Institute. Set by Bertha Goudy in Kennerley; printed by N. T. A. Munder, Baltimore. Ransom No. B-10. June.

99. THE VILLAGE TYPES

Four-page folder, 5½ x 8½ inches, announcing the manufacture of the Forum and Kennerley types by the Caslon Foundry, London. Includes line specimens of both faces. Only about 100 copies distributed, as the war prevented manufacture and shipment of type from London.

While printing, the lever of the press broke, striking Mr. Goudy a severe blow under the chin.

1914 100. ANNOUNCEMENT BY MR. LAURENCE J. GOMME

Leaf, 5 x 7¾ inches, set in Forum type; with circular reverse plate monogram 'LJG' by F. W. Goudy at top of page.

101. STEINWAY ART CASES

Booklet, 32 pages, 5⅛ x 7 inches; Japan Vellum cover, sewed with green silk. Printed in olive and black. Hand-lettering and decoration on title page, 7-line initial 'F' and headband by F. W. Goudy. Set in Kennerley by Bertha Goudy; printed by the Publishers Printing Co., New York.

102. NOW READY, KENNERLEY...FORUM TITLE

Leaf, 9 x 7 inches, announcing that the Kennerley Series, 8 to 36 pt., and the Forum Title, 10 to 36 pt., the English and Continental rights for which designs had been sold to the Caslon Foundry, London, in 1913, were now available. Prepared as an advertisement.

103. A NEW CONNECTION

Leaf, 6½ x 5⅛ inches, set in Kennerley within border No. 2409. Announces that Forum and Kennerley will be cast by H. W. Caslon & Co. of London and supplied by The Village Press and Letter Foundery.

Probably not more than 25 copies were ever issued, because only a small amount of type was available for delivery.

104. JEAN GROLIER: AN EXCERPT 1915
Broadside, 10¾ x 16½ inches, set in Kennerley and printed on Glaslan. The first work done on the Albion hand press imported from H. W. Caslon & Co. of London. Only a few copies printed. Text subsequently reprinted in *Ars Typographica*, No. 3, 1920. January 24.

105. SHIPPING LABEL
Leaf, 5 x 3¾ inches, in black; set in Forum within Village Border No. 2409. The address, 2 East 29th St., New York City, was that of the bookstore owned by Mitchell Kennerley and subsequently by Laurence J. Gomme. On Mr. Kennerley's departure, Mr. Goudy and Mr. Currier occupied the rear offices of The Little Book Shop Around The Corner.

106. TO THE GRAPHIC GROUP
Four-page folder, 7⅜ x 9⅞ inches, printed first page only, with 7-line initial 'A' by F. W. Goudy. Invitation to an informal talk by Mr. Goudy on fine printing. The American Institute of Graphic Arts admitted this group to membership. March 31.

1915

107. WHY WE HAVE CHOSEN FOREST HILLS...
  Booklet, 28 pages and cover, 6 x 9 inches; saddle stitched. Cover design in brown and green, 6-line initial 'T,' decorations, layout and text of introduction by F. W. Goudy. Set by Bertha Goudy in Kennerley and Original Old Style Italic; printed by the Commonwealth Press, New York. Ransom No. 22. April.

108. TO THE STOWAWAYS, AN INVITATION
  Leaf, 9¼ x 12 inches, in black on Arches; 8-line initial 'T' by F. W. Goudy. Set in Goudy Oldstyle (now known as Goudy Lanston) and printed on the hand press. April.

109. ANNOUNCEMENT concerning SUMMER READING
  Four-page folder, 3⅛ x 6 inches, in Kennerley and Forum; done for Mr. Laurence J. Gomme of The Little Book Shop Around The Corner. May.

110. A NOTE on LETTER-DESIGN & the VILLAGE TYPES
  Twelve-page booklet, self cover, 9 x 12 inches, on Glaslan. Includes leaf laid in, *Our Noble Art*, printed one side, with 4-line initial 'A'; headband, 8-line initial 'A' and 6-line 'B,' circular monogram 'GOUDY' on cover, all by F. W. Goudy. Fifth press mark. Ransom No. B-7. December.

A NOTE
ON LETTER-DESIGN
& THE VILLAGE TYPES

HEADING IN FORUM AND MONOGRAM BY F. W. GOUDY
(ITEM NO. 110)

111. AN OPEN LETTER FROM RICHARD LeGALLIENNE

Eight-page pamphlet, 6 x 9¼ inches, on Glaslan; sewed with white silk; 123 numbered copies signed by Mr. LeGallienne, 1,000 unnumbered with name printed. Used as Christmas gift by Mr. Gomme. Set by Bertha Goudy in Kennerley and Original Old Style Italic; printed by N. T. A. Munder, Baltimore.

A Bibliography of The Village Press

1915

112. BOOKS AS DOCTORS, BY RICHARD LeGALLIENNE
A reprint of this essay which Mr. Gomme had intended as a Christmas gift to his friends. The *Open Letter* just noted (Item No. 111) was to have served as a preface. The type was set and at least some sheets of one form (pages 13-20) were printed by Mr. Goudy on the hand press. Work was delayed, however, and time remained only to issue the *Open Letter* before the holiday. The essay was never completed.

113. A CHRISTMAS CARROLL, A POEM
Sixteen-page pamphlet, 7½ x 10 inches, on Kelmscott Crown and Sceptre; blue paper cover. An early use of Kennerley Italic; 85 copies printed on the hand press. A few copies with altered colophon were also done for Dr. Louise Acres of Chicago. December.

114. Music, by William Strode

1916

MUSIC | *By WILLIAM STRODE* | [1600-1644] | [*instrument in red*] | NEW YORK | THE VILLAGE PRESS | 1916

COLOPHON: *Music*, by William Strode, is presented to Professor Samuel A. Baldwin on May 28th, 1916; one copy only, composed and printed by Bertha M. Goudy at The Village Press, Forest Hills Gardens,

1916

New York, from types designed by Frederic W. Goudy.

PAGES: 16 [unnumbered]. Size 7½ x 11 inches.

DESIGNS: Musical instrument on title page, 2-line initial 'W' drawn in red with pen, by F. W. Goudy.

BINDING: Vellum, with 2 green silk ties; title in red on side.

EDITION: 1 copy on vellum, set in Kennerley Italic. Ransom No. 24.

COMMENT: Mrs. Goudy, a constant attendant at the concerts given by Professor Baldwin, prepared this volume, which was presented on the occasion of his 500th free organ recital at the College of the City of New York.

Fugitive Items

115. THE OATH OF HIPPOCRATES

Broadside, 16⅜ x 23½ inches, in Forum; 121 copies printed on Kelmscott Hammer and Anvil for Paul B. Hoeber for sale, plus 5 on Imperial Japan Vellum. A label with date was supplied to be affixed to the back.

Second Edition: Reprinted by Paul B. Hoeber on Hammer and Anvil in reduced size, 10¾ x 14½ inches, from a photographic reduction of the original; for sale at $1. Explanatory note printed on back.

1916 Third Edition: Facsimile reprint of the original reissued by Taylor & Taylor, San Francisco, with permission, in 1927; 500 copies done for the University of California Medical School.

116. LAURENCE J. GOMME VISITED The Village Press

Leaf, 12 x 9⅛ inches, a keepsake; with a type border and square design with lamp and book by F. W. Goudy. February 24.

117. TYPOGRAPHICA NO. 3

Pamphlet, 24 pages 8 x 10⅞ inches, self cover; in black and red on Old Stratford. Architectural design on cover, and headband and various initials by F. W. Goudy. Fifth press mark. Center spread shows Kennerley and Forum in a number of sizes.

A supplement of 4 pages (see Item No. 125) issued in October is bound into later copies.

Set by Bertha Goudy; printed by C. E. Ruckstuhl, New York. March.

118. EXHIBITION OF AMERICAN PRINTING

Poster, 11¾ x 17 inches, printed in red and black on Glaslan. Set by Bertha Goudy and printed at the Marchbanks Press, New York.

A Bibliography of The Village Press

1916

THE GETTYSBURG ADDRESS
· XIX NOVEMBER · MDCCCLXIII ·

☆

FOURSCORE & SEVEN YEARS AGO OUR FATHERS BROUGHT FORTH ON THIS CONTINENT A NEW NATION · CONCEIVED IN LIBERTY · AND DEDICATED TO THE PROPOSITION THAT ALL MEN ARE CREATED EQUAL ·
NOW WE ARE ENGAGED IN A GREAT CIVIL WAR · TESTING WHETHER THAT NATION · OR ANY NATION SO CONCEIVED AND SO DEDICATED · CAN LONG ENDURE · WE ARE MET ON A GREAT BATTLE-FIELD OF THAT WAR · WE HAVE COME TO DEDICATE A PORTION OF THAT FIELD AS A FINAL RESTING PLACE FOR THOSE WHO HERE GAVE THEIR LIVES THAT THAT NATION MIGHT LIVE · IT IS ALTOGETHER FITTING & PROPER THAT WE SHOULD DO THIS ·
BUT · IN A LARGER SENSE · WE CANNOT DEDICATE—WE CAN- NOT CONSECRATE—WE CANNOT HALLOW—THIS GROUND · THE BRAVE MEN · LIVING AND DEAD · WHO STRUGGLED HERE HAVE CONSECRATED IT FAR ABOVE OUR POOR POWER TO ADD OR DETRACT · THE WORLD WILL LITTLE NOTE NOR LONG REMEMBER WHAT WE SAY HERE · BUT IT CAN NEVER FORGET WHAT THEY DID HERE · IT IS FOR US · THE LIVING · RATHER · TO BE DEDICATED HERE TO THE UNFINISHED WORK WHICH THEY WHO FOUGHT HERE HAVE THUS FAR SO NOBLY AD- VANCED · IT IS RATHER FOR US TO BE HERE DEDICATED TO THE GREAT TASK REMAINING BEFORE US—THAT FROM THESE HONORED DEAD WE TAKE INCREASED DEVOTION TO THAT CAUSE FOR WHICH THEY GAVE THE LAST FULL MEASURE OF DEVOTION · THAT WE HERE HIGHLY RESOLVE THAT THESE DEAD SHALL NOT HAVE DIED IN VAIN · THAT THIS NATION · UNDER GOD · SHALL HAVE A NEW BIRTH OF FREEDOM · AND THAT GOVERNMENT OF THE PEOPLE · BY THE PEOPLE · FOR THE PEOPLE · SHALL NOT PERISH FROM THE EARTH ·
· ABRAHAM LINCOLN ·

119. THE GETTYSBURG ADDRESS

Broadside, 18½ x 26 inches, in Forum on Fabriano paper. Prepared for the Exhibition of American Print- ing held by the American Institute of Graphic Arts; was awarded silver medal. Less than a dozen copies printed by F. W. Goudy on the hand press, the second

1916 line of type being in the same size as the first. Second line subsequently reset smaller and printed by W. E. Rudge, Mt. Vernon, to sell for $1. Two proofs exist having the L and X of the date transposed.

Several subsequent editions were issued by Rudge. A facsimile, half-size and printed from a zinc plate, was reproduced in a trade magazine. Also reset in Forum by the Lanston Monotype Machine Co. and issued by Gimbel & Co., Philadelphia.

120. *FARNINGHAM, UNBLEACHED ARNOLD*
Four-page folder, 7½ x 11 inches, printed in brown and black. Paper sample done for the Japan Paper Co. Set by Bertha Goudy; printed by W. E. Rudge. April.

121. *FRIENDSHIP, AN ESSAY*
Eight-page pamphlet, 6 x 9 inches, containing an essay written and read at "Little Meeting," Farmington, Conn., by Marian Strong White. One copy only printed. Ransom No. 25. June.

122. GOOD NEWS TO FOREST HILLS GARDENS
Eight-page pamphlet, 6 x 9½ inches, in black and red, containing program of the celebration to be held on the 4th of July.

123. PARABLE of the WISE and FOOLISH YOUNG MEN 1916
Eight-page pamphlet, 5¾ x 8½ inches, printed in red and black; 6-line initial 'T' in red by F. W. Goudy. Set by Bertha Goudy for a customer of Brentano's and printed by C. E. Ruckstuhl, New York.

124. COMMENT ON KENNERLEY TYPE
Eight-page pamphlet, 9¼ x 12 inches, sewed with red or green silk; plus leaf laid in, *Quod si Deficiant*, in 48 pt. Forum. First showing of the 18 pt. Kennerley Italic. Fifth press mark and 6-line initial 'B' by F. W. Goudy. Set by Bertha Goudy; printed by C. E. Ruckstuhl, New York.

125. SUPPLEMENT TO TYPOGRAPHICA NO. 3
Four-page folder, 8 x 11 inches, an addition to Item No. 117; included to exhibit 3 large sizes of Kennerley roman, 2 of italic, and florets and borders. October.

126. *CONFESSIO AMANTIS*, A SONNET
Eight-page folder, 7 x 10¼ inches, French fold, in Kennerley. Some copies on Kelmscott Hammer and Anvil, others on Crown and Sceptre. A souvenir prepared by Mr. Goudy for the Society of Printers, Boston, before whom he spoke. Contains one wrong font sort; 75 copies. Ransom No. 26. December 12.

1916 127. GOODLYE DOCTRINE & INSTRUCTION
Sixteen-page booklet, 6 x 9½ inches, Etruria paper cover, title printed on side. Original Oldstyle Italic. Headband by F.W. Goudy; 50 copies printed on Glaslan for Paul B. Hoeber. Ransom No. 27. December.

128. A Personal Message

1917
A | Personal Message | Concerning Children | in War Time | From | [*here follows a list of* 39 *sponsors*] | FOUNDERS COMMITTEE | NATIONAL CHILD WELFARE ASSOCIATION, Inc. | NEW YORK | 1917

PAGES: [4] + [30 *unnumbered*] + [2]. Size 12 x 16¼ inches.

DESIGNS: Headband and 7-line initial 'F' by F.W. Goudy. Frontispiece by Louis Potter, with 14 other halftones tipped in.

BINDING: Brown boards, brown buckram back. Pasted Japanese Vellum label printed in black on side, with name of recipient of each book engrossed.

EDITION: 1,000 copies on Glaslan in red and black. Largely set by Bertha Goudy in Kennerley and Forum types. Printed by the Marchbanks Press, New York, in June.

COMMENT: The Association was about to issue this

appeal in mimeograph form when Mr. Goudy, with the greatest difficulty, persuaded them that to reach donors of sums from $1,000 to $10,000 a more arresting format was essential. It brought in over $100,000 in subscriptions.

1917

Fugitive Items

129. A PROCLAMATION by the President to the People

Broadside, 19½ x 30 inches, printed one side in red and black on Arnold Unbleached; 9-line initial 'T' in red by F. W. Goudy. Set by Bertha Goudy in Kennerley and Forum; printed for the Victor Electric Co. by the Marchbanks Press, New York. April.

130. A DECLARATION, In the Name of God, Amen

Broadside, 15¾ x 21 inches, printed one side in red, blue and black. Initial 'T' in red within typographic border; American flag, drawn by Fred Cooper, in red and blue. Set by Bertha Goudy in Kennerley; printed by the Marchbanks Press, New York. July.

131. FOREST HILLS GARDENS: Fourth Annual Celebration

Eight-page folder, 5 x 10½ inches, on Japan paper. Program of Fourth of July festivities.

1918 132. The Alphabet

THE | Alphabet | FIFTEEN | INTERPRETATIVE DESIGNS | DRAWN AND ARRANGED WITH | EXPLANATORY TEXT AND | ILLUSTRATIONS | BY | FREDERIC·W·GOUDY | [ornament] | NEW YORK | MITCHELL KENNERLEY | MCMXVIII

COLOPHON: This book has been set by Bertha M. Goudy at The Village Press, Forest Hills Gardens, New York, with types designed by the author, under whose supervision the book has been printed by William Edwin Rudge, New York City, October, 1918. The plates for the text illustrations and Alphabets were made by The Walker Engraving Co., New York City.

PAGES: [4] + 44 + [60 including 27 full-page plates]. Size 9½ x 13 inches.

DESIGNS: Circular monogram, title line, 9-line initial 'A' and numerous figures and drawings, fifth press mark; also 27 plates, each presenting 15 forms of a letter of the alphabet by F. W. Goudy.

BINDING: Black cloth; circular design containing all the letters of the alphabet in gold on side.

EDITION: 1,000 copies at $5. Set by Bertha Goudy in Kennerley and Forum; printed by W. E. Rudge.

THE Alphabet

FIFTEEN
INTERPRETATIVE DESIGNS
DRAWN AND ARRANGED WITH
EXPLANATORY TEXT AND
ILLUSTRATIONS

BY
FREDERIC·W·GOUDY

NEW YORK
MITCHELL KENNERLEY
MCMXVIII

1918 COMMENT: The dedication to Mrs. Goudy was included without her knowledge, a matter of no small difficulty, as Mrs. Goudy set the whole text and corrected the proof. This explains the unusual position of the dedication, for the customary space could not have been left open without an explanation to her.

The second edition, published in 1922, may be distinguished by the last line of the frontispiece which is black in the original and red in the second edition, and by the date MCMXXII on the title page. A third edition was printed in April, 1926, without, however, changing the date on the title page. A fourth edition notes the change from Mitchell Kennerley to William Edwin Rudge as publisher, and bears the date 1932.

Fugitive Items

133. A TRIBUTE TO OUR FALLEN AVIATORS

Full-page architectural design by F. W. Goudy, 9¼ x 12¼ inches, with 8 lines of text in Forum set by Bertha Goudy.

134. ARS TYPOGRAPHICA, NUMBER ONE

Magazine, 52 pages, 8¼ x 12½ inches, brown paper cover printed in brown and black. Frontispiece in gravure, a photograph of the Kelmscott Press taken by

Mr. Goudy. Reduced reproduction of 2 trial pages of Morris's *Froissart's Chronicles*. Numerous other reproductions, headbands and initials. Contains first showing of the Hadriano type of F. W. Goudy (page 36), which page was set by Bertha Goudy. Balance of the composition in Kennerley. Printed on Old Stratford Laid Antique by the Marchbanks Press, New York, who did the balance of the composition. Price $1. May.

1918

COVER OF FIRST ISSUE OF "ARS TYPOGRAPHICA"

Ars Typographica

Volume I   Summer 1918   Number 2

HEADING FROM SECOND ISSUE OF "ARS TYPOGRAPHICA"

135. ARS TYPOGRAPHICA, NUMBER TWO
Magazine, 48 pages, 8¼ x 12½ inches, brown paper cover printed in blue and black. Set in Goudy Modern, its first showing, with headings in Goudy Open. Composition and printing, on Old Stratford, by the Marchbanks Press, New York. Price $1. October.

136. PROSPECTUS FOR *THE ALPHABET*
Four-page folder, 9½ x 12½ inches, on Alexandra Japan, reproducing title page and plate of the letter 'G.' Circular monogram and 9-line initial 'T' by F.W. Goudy. Set by Bertha Goudy in Kennerley; printed by W. E. Rudge, New York.

137. EXHIBITION OF PICTORIAL PHOTOGRAPHS
Eight-page folder, 4⅝ x 8½ inches. Circular device of winged horse on cover is not by Mr. Goudy. About 500 copies done for Columbia. November 11-30.

138. Art and the Great War 1919

ART [*in brown*] | AND THE GREAT WAR | *By* | ALBERT EUGENE GALLATIN | [*8 lines of offices held*] | *With One Hundred Illustrations* | [*fleuron in brown*] | NEW YORK | E.P. DUTTON & COMPANY | 1919

COLOPHON: This book has been set by Bertha M. Goudy from types and decorations designed by Frederick W. Goudy and printed in the shop of William E. Rudge, New York City. The engravings were made by the Beck Engraving Company, New York City.

PAGES: [2] + 228 + [66]. Size 9½ x 12½ inches.

DESIGNS: Headband, 8-line initial 'W' in brown by F. W. Goudy. Text contains 100 full-page halftone and line illustrations on coated stock. Three are in full color, tipped in opposite the chapter openings.

BINDING: Green paper-covered boards, green cloth back. Hand-lettered title in gold on side.

EDITION: Set by Bertha Goudy in Kennerley, and printed by W. E. Rudge, New York.

COMMENT: The colophon must have been set at the printer's, for it spells Mr. Goudy's first name 'Frederick.' One copy contains Mr. Goudy's written note: "I never spell my name with a 'k.' I am sure my wife knows my name, but there it is!"

1919 139. Faculty, College of Physicians & Surgeons

THE FACULTY | OF THE | COLLEGE OF PHYSICIANS & SURGEONS | COLUMBIA UNIVERSITY IN THE CITY | OF NEW YORK | *TWENTY-FOUR PORTRAITS* | *By* | DORIS U. JAEGER | WITH A FOREWORD BY SAMUEL W. LAMBERT | M.D., A.B., A.M., PH.B. | [*monogram 'D.U.J.'*] | NEW YORK | PAUL B. HOEBER | 1919

PAGES: [16] + [*24 full-page portraits unnumbered*]. Size 10 x 14 inches.

DESIGNS: Monogram on title page, headband and 8-line initial 'A' by F.W. Goudy.

BINDING: Blue boards, white linen back; title in gold on side.

EDITION: Set by Bertha Goudy in Kennerley; printed by the Marchbanks Press on Hammer and Anvil.

COMMENT: The title page was set personally by Mr. Goudy.

140. The Song of Songs

THE | SONG OF SONGS | WHICH IS SOLOMON'S

COLOPHON: Twenty-one copies have been printed and bound for their friends, by Frederic and Bertha Goudy, at The Village Press, Forest Hills Gardens, New York. Christmas, 1919.

PAGES: [2] + 11 + [3]. Size 10¼ x 14½ inches.
DESIGNS: Various initials and circular rose by F. W. Goudy.

BINDING: Gray boards, title with circular monogram on side.

EDITION: 21 copies on Italian watermarked paper; 1 copy on vellum. Kennerley type. Ransom No. 28.

COMMENT: The single vellum copy was printed without initials for Mr. Haskell Coffin, who illuminated it for presentation to Miss Frances Starr. The 21 paper copies were for distribution to friends of The Village Press.

Fugitive Item

141. DIGNITY

Twelve-page pamphlet, 6¼ x 9¼ inches, French fold cover. Monogram 'S. P. Co.' on title page, headband and 5-line initial 'A' by F. W. Goudy. Set by Bertha Goudy; printed on Old Stratford Book by the F. A. Bassette Co., Springfield, Mass., for Strathmore Paper Co.

Originally designed considerably larger. Awarded a medal at the second exhibition of printing of the American Institute of Graphic Arts at the National Arts Club, May, 1920.

1920 142. An Appreciation: Elmer Adler

AN | APPRECIATION | OF THE WORK | OF | ELMER ADLER | MCMXX

COLOPHON: Four copies only of this tribute to Elmer Adler, written by McAllister Coleman, have been printed in October, 1920, at the shop of William Edwin Rudge, in types designed by Fred W. Goudy.

PAGES: [4] + [9 unnumbered] + [3]. Size 8 x 12¼ inches.

DESIGNS: A 7-line initial 'O,' illuminated in red and gold by F. W. Goudy.

BINDING: Blue boards, brown leather back. Vellum copy, full black leather for presentation to Mr. Adler.

EDITION: 3 copies on Glaslan, 1 on vellum. Set by Bertha Goudy in Kennerley and Forum; printed by W. E. Rudge, New York. October.

Fugitive Items

143. PRINTING EXHIBITION, MAY 5 TO JUNE 1

Poster in 2 sizes, 14 x 19¾ and 9 x 12¼ inches, printed in black with Aldus medallions in red-brown. Set in Forum with a type unit border. Announces an Exhibition of the American Institute of Graphic Arts at the National Arts Club. Awarded gold medal.

144. VALUABLE DOCUMENTS—CRANE'S 1920
French fold leaflet, 8 x 10⅝ inches, printed in black with blue rules on unglazed bond; cover in blue with all-around border on Mazarine glazed. Border and 7-line initial 'T' by F. W. Goudy. Set by Bertha Goudy in Goudy Antique type; 2,150 copies printed by the Marchbanks Press, New York, for Crane & Co. June.

145. FACSIMILE TRIAL PAGES: *Froissart's Chronicles*
Four-page folder, 11⅛ x 16⅜ inches, printed in red and black, reproducing 2 facing pages from the edition projected by William Morris. In stiff folder, green paper boards, white linen back, pasted label on side. Note on first page in Goudy Lanston set by Bertha Goudy; 110 copies printed by W. E. Rudge, New York, on Japan Vellum for F. W. Goudy, intended to sell at $5.

An additional run on Japan Vellum and about 100 copies on Kelmscott were printed by Mr. Rudge for his own use, which determined Mr. Goudy to give up the idea of selling his and to give them away instead.

146. TO THE RESIDENTS OF FOREST HILLS GARDENS
Four-page folder, 12¼ x 17 inches, printed in red and black on Glaslan. Independence Day Proclamation with 7-line initial 'O' in red by F. W. Goudy and

1920 (on page 3) *The American's Creed* by Wm. Tyler Page, set in Forum (see also page 36, *Ars Typographica*, No. II, 1918). Set by Bertha Goudy; printed by W. E. Rudge, New York. Ransom No. B-11. July.

147. ARS TYPOGRAPHICA, NUMBER THREE

Magazine, 50 pages, 8¼ x 12½ inches, light brown paper cover printed in red and black. Headband, 7-line initial 'A' and press mark of the Marchbanks Press by F. W. Goudy. Reproduction of large biblical initial 'G' used on Christmas greeting in 1913 (Item No. 93).

Contains a leaf, *Le Bonheur de ce Monde, Sonnet, Composé par Christoph Plantin,* set by Bertha Goudy in Garamond and printed on Arches on the hand press to accompany and illustrate an article by Mr. Goudy — *Hand-Press Printing: A Plea for a Lost Craft.* The old-style long 's' forms were made from lowercase 'f's. After about 300 copies were printed, the furniture contracted and the type pied. As some 500 of the 1,000 copies of the magazine were being bound at once, the Marchbanks Press reprinted the leaf with this note: "This insert was printed on a John Thomson Press. Goudy pied his form and we have no hand press."

Balance of magazine set in Caslon No. 471 and

printed on Old Stratford by the Marchbanks Press, New York. Price $1.50. Dated on cover SPRING 1920; on first page of text WINTER 1920; on contents page SPRING 1920; in colophon JUNE 1920. Ransom No. B-13.

PRESS MARK OF THE MARCHBANKS PRESS, BY F. W. GOUDY
(FROM ITEM NO. 147)

148. FOREST HILLS GARDENS BULLETIN

Eight-page folder, 8½ x 11½ inches. First page only set at The Village Press in Kennerley. A note on page 5 headed *Art Typography* reads: "The first page of this special edition of the July Fourth Bulletin has been set by Bertha M. Goudy in types designed and arranged by Frederic W. Goudy." June.

A Bibliography of The Village Press

1920 149. AN ART DIRECTOR FOR THE MONOTYPE
Four-page folder, 7½ x 12 inches; 9-line initial 'T' in red by F. W. Goudy, who also wrote the text. Set by Bertha Goudy in Suburban French; printed by the Lanston Monotype Machine Co., Philadelphia. December.

1921 150. PLACE CARDS
Series of 10 to 12 folders, each 4 pages, 5⅜ x 8¾ inches, used as place cards at a dinner given by Mr. and Mrs. Goudy, March 28th, to Miss Pamela Bianco. Large circular floral monogram 'GOUDY' with the name of a guest on the first page. The third page contained a poem, each copy different.

151. PHILOBIBLON: A RICARDO DE BURY SCRIPTUM
Leaf, 8½ x 11 inches; first trial impressions of the Goudy Newstyle before modifications. April 22.

152. THE CRAFTSMAN'S IDEAL
Leaf, 9 x 12¼ inches, on Warren's Olde Style; 7-line initial 'B' by F. W. Goudy, who also wrote the text. Set by Bertha Goudy in Newstyle type "designed . . . for use in his forthcoming *Typologia*." Printed by the Marchbanks Press, New York, for the Craftsman's Number of *The American Printer*, July. May 27.

153. A SPECIMEN OF TYPES   1921
   Broadside, 13¼ x 21½ inches, in red and black on Crane's Bond (a few on Japan). Specimen of types designed by F. W. Goudy set by Bertha Goudy; printed by Marchbanks Press. Ransom No. B-14. September.

154. PHILOBIBLON: A RICARDO DE BURY SCRIPTUM
   Leaf, 10¼ x 14¾ inches, similar to Item No. 151 but in narrower measure, with fleuron and altered note. About 25 copies done for the Stowaways. October 22.

155. IN THE WAKE OF THE STOWAWAYS
   Proofs, 7½ x 10¾ inches, of trial pages of a volume (never issued) of Stowaway history. Forum and Newstyle; 13-line initial 'A' not by Mr. Goudy. October.

156. THE AMERICAN INSTITUTE OF GRAPHIC ARTS
   Broadside, 10½ x 14½ inches, in red and black. Objects of the Institute, with officers. Honorary President, Walter Gilliss; President, F. W. Goudy. Undated.

157. A COMMUNICATION FROM THE PRESIDENT
   Projected 4-page folder, 8¾ x 12½ inches. A message from F. W. Goudy, new president of A. I. G. A., to the members. Seven-line initial 'A' by F. W. Goudy. Set by Bertha Goudy in Newstyle; never completed.

1922 158. Elements of Lettering

ELEMENTS OF | LETTERING | [WITH XIII FULL-PAGE PLATES] | By | FREDERIC W. GOUDY | *Author of* THE ALPHABET. *Editor,* ARS TYPOGRAPHICA | Text composed by BERTHA M. GOUDY in types | designed by the Author | [*circular floral monogram* 'GOUDY'] | NEW YORK : MITCHELL KENNERLEY | 1922

COLOPHON: This manual has been set by Bertha M. Goudy at The Village Press, Forest Hills Gardens, New York, with types designed by the author, and printed under his supervision at the Marchbanks Press, New York City, in May, 1922. Published by Mitchell Kennerley, New York.

PAGES: [10] + 48 + [10]. Size 9½ x 12½ inches.

DESIGNS: Circular monogram, numerous figures and designs, headband and 7-line initial 'T' by F. W. Goudy, besides 13 full-page plates.

BINDING: Green cloth, title in gold on side; slip case.

EDITION: 1,000 copies at $5. Set by Bertha Goudy in Kennerley, and printed at the Marchbanks Press.

COMMENT: Professor C. Lauron Hooper, to whom this book is dedicated, was Mr. Goudy's associate and partner in his earliest printing venture, the Booklet Press (see page 7).

ELEMENTS OF LETTERING

⁋Regarding Letters in General

THE hypothesis that there is an ideally *correct* form for each letter of the alphabet is just as erroneous as Geofroy Tory's* simple assumption that there is a relation between the shapes of letters & the human body; erroneous, because the shapes of letters have been in constant process of modification from their very beginnings. Indeed, the shapes of the letters in daily use are due entirely to a convention, so that in preferring one form rather than another, our only consideration need be for the conventions now existing and the degree in which each satisfies our sense of beauty.

It should be kept clearly in mind that "the perfect model of a letter is altogether imaginary and arbitrary. There is a

---

*Geofroy Tory [1480-1532], *Imprimeur du Roi*, painter, engraver and author, in his book *Champfleury* on the correct proportions of letters, "at once the most useless, most curious work on lettering in existence," sought to derive the capital letters from the Goddess IO, these two letters furnishing the perpendicular and circle from which all letters were to be formed to measurements proportioned to the human body.

1922 159. Kidd: A Moral Opuscule

KIDD: | A MORAL OPUSCULE | The Verse [sic] by | Richard J. | Walsh | Illustrations [sick] | by George | Illian | [ship in color between double horizontal rules] | NEW YORK: William Edwin Rudge | 1922

COLOPHON: [Colophony Note] Executed (hung up) at the Printing House of Billo Rudge, Mount Vernon, New York, during the summer of 1922. The Press Gang assisting at the execution comprised the following notorious persons: Richard J. Walsh, B. V. D. (Doctor of Bad Verse); George Illian, D. U. D. (Doctor of Underdone Design); Fred W. Goudy, T. D. (Typothetic Designer); Bertha M. Goudy, C. E. (Compositrice Extraordinaire); Bruce Rogers, L. O. M. (Lay-out Man); Frank S. Goerke, L. U. M. (Lock-up Man); Paul J. Peters, R. I. P. (Reader of Incoherent Proof); Thomas C. Hughes, M. P. (Master of the Press); Edith Diehl, B. B. (Book Bindress); Frank Branca, P. S. (Packer and Shipper). Hic et Nunc (Especially Hic).

PAGES: [4] + [22 unnumbered] + [2]. Size 7 x 9¼ inches.

DESIGNS: Hand-colored drawings by George Illian.

BINDING: Magenta Japan Vellum boards, green label on side.

EDITION: Designed by Bruce Rogers. Set by Bertha 1922
Goudy in Newstyle; printed on Tarazona by W. E.
Rudge, Mount Vernon.

COMMENT: "Dick Walsh, then editor of *Colliers'*, wrote the verse. We furnished the set type to Rudge in galleys and Rudge made up and printed the book. The late George Illian made the drawings—the whole thing a bit of delightful foolery."—F.W.G.

160. A Book of Portraits

A BOOK OF | PORTRAITS | OF THE FACULTY OF | THE MEDICAL DEPARTMENT OF THE | JOHNS HOPKINS UNIVERSITY | BALTIMORE | By | DORIS ULMANN | [*seal of the University in red*] | BALTIMORE, MD. | THE JOHNS HOPKINS PRESS | 1922

COLOPHON: [*On copyright page*] Printed at the shop of William E. Rudge, Mount Vernon, N.Y. Type composition by Bertha M. Goudy at The Village Press, Forest Hills Gardens, N.Y., in Newstyle types designed by Frederic W. Goudy.

PAGES: [6] + [*82 unnumbered*] + [2]. Size 10¼ x 15⅜ inches.

DESIGNS: Title line, headband and 7-line initial 'A' by F.W. Goudy; 36 full-page portraits in photogravure, and frontispiece of the University.

1922   BINDING: Blue boards, white buckram back. Seal of the University in gold on side.

EDITION: Set by Bertha Goudy in Newstyle and printed by W. E. Rudge, Mount Vernon.

Fugitive Items

161. PROSPECTUS FOR *ELEMENTS OF LETTERING*

Four-page folder, 8½ x 11 inches, on Alexandra Japan, announcing *Elements of Lettering* and the second edition of *The Alphabet*. Set by Bertha Goudy in Kennerley; printed by the Marchbanks Press, New York.

162. NEWS FROM THE PRINTERS' PARADISE

Four-page folder, 8½ x 11 inches, an invitation to a meeting of the American Institute of Graphic Arts. Mr. Goudy, then President of the Institute, was the speaker. A 9-line initial 'M' in orange by F. W. Goudy, who also wrote the text. Set by Bertha Goudy in the Goudy Lanston; printed on Kelmscott Hammer and Anvil by N. T. A. Munder, Baltimore. February 15.

163. ANNUAL REPORT, LANSTON MONOTYPE...

Sixteen-page booklet, 6x9¼ inches, brown French fold cover printed in brown and black. Report for the year ending Feb. 28, 1922. Six-line initial 'I' by F. W.

Goudy. President's Report set by Bertha Goudy in Goudy Garamont, No. 248, its first use; printed on Japan Vellum by Thomsen-Ellis Co., Baltimore. May 4. **1922**

164. MIRABEAU'S TRIBUTE TO BENJAMIN FRANKLIN **1923**
Leaf, 8¾ x 11¾ inches, contributed to the Franklin Bi-Centennial Number of *The American Printer*. Set by Bertha Goudy in Garamont, the first use of the 12 pt.; printed and donated by the Currier Press, New York.

165. HONORARY PRESIDENT OF THE A. I. G. A.
Four-page folder, 12 x 16½ inches on Swedish handmade, with signed gravure reproduction laid in of a photograph of Mr. Goudy by Clarence H. White. The eighth keepsake of the American Institute of Graphic Arts, written by E. G. Gress. Goudy Newstyle type. Ransom No. B-16. March.

166. AMERICAN INSTITUTE OF GRAPHIC ARTS
Leaf, 7 x 9¼ inches. Note of transmittal to accompany Keepsake No. 8 (Item No. 165). Headband and 6-line initial 'W' by F. W. Goudy. Set in Kennerley and printed damp on Rives. Ransom No. B-17. April.

THE VILLAGE PRESS AND LETTER FOUNDERY IN THE OLD MILL, 1938
DEEPDENE, MARLBOROUGH, N.Y. (PHOTO BY CHARLES E. PONT)

PUBLICATIONS OF THE VILLAGE PRESS
AT MARLBOROUGH, NEW YORK
from  1923

A Note on the Albion Hand-press, No. 6551
[BY FREDERIC W. GOUDY]

When William Morris selected the hand-press for his printing, he set himself certain limitations—limitations, yes; but not those under which the ordinary printer works. He decided that if he used a "machine" (as a power press is called in England) he would have to plan his books in such a way as to bring them within the capabilities of the machine, and he felt that facilities of production and speed would not compensate for restrictions in choice of paper, ink and quality of impression. He reasoned that, if he must think of his books as limited by the machine, he was exalting the mere instrument of production as an end, instead of a means to an end. With the hand-press he could maintain hand work—that is, he would use it as a tool

1924 with a minimum of anything intervening between the hand and its work.

In my introductory pages to this volume I have spoken of the Schneidewend & Lee hand-press with which The Village Press began work. I have no doubt that some of my feeling at that time *might* have been the same as Morris's regarding the use of the hand-press, but I very much doubt whether either Ransom or myself had reached that stage then, since neither of us had ever attempted to master the idiosyncrasies of such a tool. I rather imagine that the actual reason was the matter of expense; we *could* buy a hand-press and we *could not* acquire a power press adequate for the quality of work we determined to make our sine qua non.

When I learned early in 1924 through my friend Gress* that James Guthrie was the owner of one of the hand-presses actually used by Morris and that he would consider selling it, I cabled at once asking the price at which he was holding it. With customary English conservatism I duly received (by mail) a reply, and in a few days a cheque was on its way to him.

In March of the same year the press arrived at Cus-

*The late Edmund G. Gress, Editor of *The American Printer*.

toms and the customs people, fearing an influx of 1924
Morris presses would work hardship to American
printers, fined us for duty an amount that would buy
a new press identical with it, pay freight and duty,
too. With duty paid the press was temporarily lodged
in the exhibition rooms of the Anderson Galleries,
and on it my wife and I printed a slim booklet, Edna
St. Vincent Millay's *Renascence,* for sale to visitors to
the exhibition. At the same time some Village Press
items also were exhibited.

Following this exhibition the press was set up in
our workshop at Marlborough. The most important
bit of printing done on it was the *Three Essays* by Augustine Birrell for the Grolier Club's Printers' Series
(and not too well done, either).

I was glad to find, on examining the press, that it
was the one on which the two trial pages of the Kelmscott *Froissart,* of which I had a copy on vellum, were
printed. William Morris employed in all three Albion
presses, but this particular one, No. 6551, dated 1891, is
unmistakably distinguished by two heavy iron bands
sweated on, one on each side, a reinforcement necessitated by the large pages of the Press's most monumental achievement, the Kelmscott *Chaucer.*

A Bibliography of The Village Press

1924   In a letter written by Sir Emery Walker in April, 1932, just before he died, to my friend Melbert B. Cary, Jr., the present owner of the press, he described it as follows:

"Morris had a number of presses and they were all sold when the Press was closed in 1898. From the dimensions you give and the fact that the press was reinforced with iron bands makes me think that it might be one of Morris's presses which were made for the printing of the *Chaucer*. The impression of the two pages together was very heavy and I remember the bands being added for extra strength."

Before this press came into my possession it passed through a number of hands and was employed in a variety of work. Its interesting history has been included with a hitherto unpublished essay by William Morris, *Some Thoughts on the Ornamented MSS. of the Middle Ages*, in a book issued by Mr. Cary at the Press of the Woolly Whale and printed on Morris's press on the 100th anniversary of Morris's birth, March 24, 1934.

My acquisition of this press should be sufficient reason to insure for The Village Press a very definite mention in the annals of American printing. I parted with it with extreme reluctance; it was an expensive

FREDERIC W. GOUDY WITH THE WILLIAM MORRIS PRESS
AT THE ANDERSON GALLERIES, NEW YORK
(PHOTO BY ARNOLD GENTHE, N.Y.)

1924 luxury, one that I could not afford, and the demands on my time in other directions seemed to preclude any except very occasional use, so when Spencer Kellogg made me an offer which covered my investment in it, I decided to give it up.

167. Three Essays

Three Essays: [*hand-lettered in outline*] | I · BOOK-BUYING ·· II · BOOK-BINDING | III · THE OFFICE OF LITERATURE | BY | AUGUSTINE BIRRELL | [*fleuron*] | NEW YORK · THE GROLIER CLUB | M·CM·XXIV

COLOPHON: The *Three Essays* by Augustine Birrell have been printed by Frederic and Bertha Goudy at The Village Press, Marlborough-on-Hudson, New York. Composed by Mrs. Goudy with types designed by Mr. Goudy and printed on the Albion hand-press formerly owned and used by William Morris at the Kelmscott Press, Hammersmith, England.

Book-buying, and *The Office of Literature* are reprinted from *Obiter Dicta*, published by Duckworth & Co., London. *Book-binding* is from *Men, Women and Books*, copyright, 1894, by Charles Scribner's Sons, New York, and is here reprinted with their kind permission.

Finished December, 1924.

PAGES: [10] + xxvi + [8]. Size 8¼ x 11½ inches.   1924
DESIGNS: Title line hand-lettered by F. W. Goudy.
BINDING: Blue boards, cloth back; title on printed label pasted on side.
EDITION: 300 copies on Grolier Hand-made. Goudy Newstyle type. Ransom No. 29.
COMMENT: This is the 6th and last volume in the Grolier Club's American Printers' Series. The first book to be printed by Mr. Goudy on the William Morris hand-press after its arrival in Marlborough.

Fugitive Items

168. THIS KEEPSAKE IS THE FIRST IMPRESSION...

Leaf, 8½ x 11¾ inches, on Kelmscott Hammer and Anvil. Set by Bertha Goudy in Kennerley Italic, with 5th press mark, within a border drawn by Morris to surround a Burne-Jones illustration in the Kelmscott *Chaucer*, reproduced from the original drawing owned by Mr. Goudy. Printed damp on the William Morris hand-press, just received from England and on exhibition at the Anderson Galleries, New York. These keepsakes, the first impressions to be pulled in America, were printed and distributed to visitors. (Reproduced on page 160). Ransom No. B-18. March.

KEEPSAKE PRODUCED ON THE MORRIS HAND-PRESS
DURING AN EXHIBITION AT THE ANDERSON GALLERIES, NEW YORK
(ITEM NO. 168)

169. RENASCENCE, A POEM BY EDNA ST. V. MILLAY   1924
Sixteen-page booklet, 3⅞ x 9 inches, blue paper cover sewed with white silk. Only the title page and colophon set by Bertha Goudy; the balance in Garamont by the Monotype Co. Printed by F. W. Goudy on the William Morris hand-press while on exhibition at the Anderson Galleries, New York. Bound by Bertha Goudy and sold only during the exhibition at $2. Less than 200 copies issued, numbered and initialed by F. W. Goudy. March.

170. MR. and MRS. F. W. GOUDY CORDIALLY INVITE…
Four-page folder, 6½ x 10 inches, on Arches. Invitation to the Stowaways to visit The Village Press and Letter Foundery. Set in an early cutting of Italian Old Style. July 26.

171. The Lark Ascending   1925

The | LARK ASCENDING | BY | *GEORGE MEREDITH* | MARLBOROUGH-ON-HUDSON | FREDERIC & BERTHA GOUDY | MARCH 8, 1925

COLOPHON: This poem, *The Lark Ascending,* by George Meredith, has been printed and bound by Frederic and Bertha Goudy, at The Village Press,

1925 Marlborough-on-Hudson, New York, one copy only, for Professor Samuel A. Baldwin, March 8th, 1925.

PAGES: [8] + [5 leaves] + [6]. Size 7½ x 11 inches.
BINDING: Vellum, with 2 gray silk ties.
EDITION: 1 copy only on Crown and Sceptre. Set in Kennerley Italic.
COMMENT: Issued on the occasion of the 1,000th organ recital given by Professor Baldwin at the College of the City of New York. Mrs. Goudy had attended some 700 of the concerts. A previous commemorative volume, *Music,* had been presented by Mr. and Mrs. Goudy in 1916 (Item No. 114) at Professor Baldwin's 500th recital.

172. [A Book of Signatures]

Volume of blank pages, 10 x 14¾ inches, ruled for the signatures of those attending the 1,000th free organ recital, given by Professor Samuel A. Baldwin on March 8. Contains introductory page, 16 lines of text set by Bertha Goudy in Forum, reading in part: "We whose names are here inscribed wish thereby to express our appreciation of the ever kind and generous service of Professor Samuel A. Baldwin who... has freely bestowed his great art and wide knowledge..."

173. A Portrait Gallery   1925

A | Portrait Gallery | OF AMERICAN EDITORS | BEING | A GROUP OF XLIII LIKENESSES | BY | DORIS ULMANN | WITH CRITICAL ESSAYS BY THE EDITORS | AND AN INTRODUCTION | BY | LOUIS EVAN SHIPMAN | [type ornament] | NEW YORK | WILLIAM EDWIN RUDGE | 1925

COLOPHON: [Follows copyright page] William Edwin Rudge certifies that this copy of *A Portrait Gallery of American Editors* by Doris Ulmann is one of an edition of 375 copies, of which 350 only are for sale. The types, designed and arranged by Frederic W. Goudy, have been set by Bertha M. Goudy at The Village Press, Marlborough-on-Hudson, New York. Presswork by William Edwin Rudge, Mount Vernon, New York. This is No.—

PAGES: [18] + 177 + [7]. Size 11½ x 16 inches.

DESIGNS: An 8-line initial 'T' by F. W. Goudy; 43 full-page portraits in photogravure.

BINDING: Blue boards, buckram back. Title in gold on side.

EDITION: 375 copies, 350 for sale at $35. Set by Bertha Goudy in Italian Old Style; printed on Rives by W. E. Rudge, Mount Vernon.

1925 *Fugitive Items*

174. JOHN A. STAPLES WISHES YOU...

Christmas folder, 4 pages, 5 x 7½ inches, printed first page only. Photogravure of residence in green, and 5 lines of Marlborough capitals, constituting the first use of this type.

1926
175. TYPOGRAPHICA NO. 4

Thirty-six-page pamphlet, 8¼ x 11¾ inches, gray-green paper cover. Frontispiece in photogravure of the Village Letter Foundery at Deepdene. Various initial letters and ornaments by F. W. Goudy. Contains showings of 17 faces cast and for sale by Mr. Goudy, and full-page advertisement for *Ars Typographica*, new series, published by Douglas C. McMurtrie. The word 'Typographica' on the title page is from the first casting done at the Foundery. Set by Bertha Goudy and printed on Dacian. July.

176. IMPORTANT ANNOUNCEMENT TO PRINTERS

Four-page folder, 6¼ x 9½ inches, offering for sale type from the Village Letter Foundery and announcing as ready *Typographica No. 4*. Five-line initial 'O' by F. W. Goudy. Set in Newstyle; about 200 copies were printed, but never issued.

177. TYPOGRAPHICA NO. 5   1927

Thirty-two-page pamphlet, 8 x 11⅞ inches, green paper cover. Displays 25 type faces and various borders produced by the Village Letter Foundery. Third press mark. Set by Bertha Goudy and Peter Beilenson; printed by D. C. McMurtrie, New York. Prepared for Continental Typefounders Association, Inc. Summer.

178. WORTHY PAPERS

Eight-page folder, 3⅞ x 6¼ inches, French fold, in red and black. The first work done in Deepdene type. Set by Bertha Goudy; printed by the Walpole Printing Office, New Rochelle. Prepared for distribution by the Worthy Paper Co. at the Graphic Arts Exposition, Sept. 5-17, New York.

179. DEEPDENE: A NEW TYPE

Broadside, 11½ x 16 inches, printed both sides in red and black. A presentation of the Deepdene type; line specimens of 4 sizes of roman on back. Six-line initial 'L' in red by F.W. Goudy. Set by Peter Beilenson at The Village Press; a few copies on Hadrian printed by Mr. Goudy on the hand-press; balance of edition printed on Berkshire Text by the L. F. White Co., New York. The first type that Mr. Goudy person-

1927 ally cut in several related sizes. Prepared for the use of Continental Typefounders Association, Inc., at the Graphic Arts Exposition, Sept. 5-17, New York.

> DEEPDENE: A NEW TYPE PRODUCED IN EVERY DETAIL BY THE DESIGNER OF THE FACE · NOW FIRST OFFERED TO PRINTERS · SEPT · MCMXXVII
>
> ETTER-Cutting is a Handy-Work hitherto kept ſo conceal'd among the Artificers of it, that I˙ cannot learn anyone hath taught it to any other; But every one that has uſed it, Learnt it of his own Genuine Inclination. Therefore, though I cannot [as in other trades] deſcribe the general Practice of Work-men, yet the Rules I follow I ſhall ſhew here.... For, indeed, by the appearance of ſome Work done, a judicious Eye may doubt whether they go by any Rule at all, though Geometrick Rules, in no Practice whatever, ought to be more nicely or exactly obſerved than in this.
>
> FROM DEEPDENE BROADSIDE, SHOWING INITIAL BY MR. GOUDY

180. INTERNATIONAL TYPOGRAPHIC COUNCIL

Leaf, 10⅛ x 8⅝ inches, in Hadriano with type unit border. Keepsake, issued on the occasion of the visit of members to The Village Press. The first use of the 18 pt. Hadriano. September 17.

181. THE COMPLIMENTS OF THE SEASON

Four-page folder, 6½ x 10 inches. Christmas greetings, set in Companion Old Style, a private type cut for *The Woman's Home Companion*, printed on Arches. Contains tipped-in halftone, *The Cascade at Deepdene*.

182. Two Singers   1928

TWO | *SINGERS* | By | CHARLES HANSON TOWNE | [*fleuron*] | NEW YORK: WILLIAM EDWIN RUDGE | 1928

COLOPHON: Three hundred and fifty copies of this book, each signed by the author, were printed at The Village Press, Marlborough-on-Hudson, New York, from types designed by Frederic W. Goudy and set by Bertha M. Goudy. July, Mcmxxviii.

PAGES: [10] + [16 *unnumbered*] + [6]. Size 6¼ x 9¼ inches.

BINDING: Blue boards, brown cloth back. Title in gold on side.

EDITION: 350 copies at $6 printed on Glaslan; set in Deepdene.

COMMENT: Published by W. E. Rudge.

183. The World's Lincoln

THE | WORLD'S LINCOLN | By | JOHN DRINKWATER | [*type ornament*] | NEW YORK | THE BOWLING GREEN PRESS | 1928

COLOPHON: Eight hundred copies of *The World's Lincoln* by John Drinkwater has been set in August, 1927, by Bertha M. Goudy at The Village Press, Marlborough-on-Hudson, N.Y., in types designed by Fred-

1928 eric W. Goudy. Presswork and binding at the Printing House of William Edwin Rudge, Mount Vernon, N.Y.

PAGES: [4] + 34 + [6]. Size 6 x 9 inches.

DESIGNS: 6-line initial 'S' in brown by F. W. Goudy.

BINDING: Blue boards, white vellum back. Title in gold on side.

EDITION: 800 copies; set by Bertha Goudy in the Marlborough type and printed on Arches by W. E. Rudge, Mount Vernon.

COMMENT: Published by the Bowling Green Press.

Fugitive Items

184. MONOTYPE, GOUDY NUMBER

Magazine, 16 pages, 9 x 11⅞ inches, self cover. Full-page portrait of F. W. Goudy and hand-lettered line, *Art in Type Design*. Set by Bertha Goudy in various Goudy Monotype faces, the text in Goudy Lanston (formerly called Goudy Antique, originally Goudy Oldstyle; see Item No. 81 for its first use). November.

185. THE SEASON'S GREETINGS...

Four-page folder, 5¾ x 3¼ inches, printed first page only. Christmas card, set in Goudy Text, an early use, with 3-line initial 'T' by F. W. Goudy.

186. TRIAL IMPRESSION OF DEEPDENE ITALIC 1929
Four-page folder, 9 x 12¾ inches, showing 2 pages of text, set in Deepdene Italic by Bertha Goudy. The matrices for this showing in 24 pt. were engraved by Bertha Goudy. February.

187. OLD STRATFORD BOOK PAPERS
Forty-four-page booklet, 6¼ x 9¼ inches, white paper cover printed in brown and black. Paper sample book made up of numerous signatures in various colors, set in different types, including Marlborough, Goudy Modern, Deepdene Roman and Italic, Italian Old Style, Poliphilus and Strathmore Title. The last, cut for this booklet and never used elsewhere, appears on the cover and title page in 30 and 36 pt., the only sizes made. Reproduces page 34 from *The World's Lincoln*, and *Confessio Amantis* (Item No. 126). A 7-line initial 'A' in olive by F. W. Goudy. Set by Bertha Goudy and printed by the Strathmore Paper Co.

188. GUTENBERG'S INVENTION
Broadside, 11⅜ x 14⅜ inches, printed one side in black with red added by hand. Christmas poem on Rives, set in 11 different types and relating *The True Amazing Story of the Invention of Printing*.

1929 189. CHRISTMAS, MCMXXIX
Four-page folder, 5 x 7½ inches, printed first page only. About 100 copies done for Louise Acres, Mrs. Goudy's physician.

190. Rip Van Winkle

1930 WASHINGTON IRVING [underscored] | RIP VAN WIN-KLE | A POSTHUMOUS WRITING | OF | DIEDRICH KNICKERBOCKER | *With an Introduction* | BY | MARK VAN DOREN | [monogram 'L.E.C.' in brown] | THE LIMITED EDITIONS CLUB | NEW YORK · MCMXXX

COLOPHON: This ends the text of the first edition of *Rip Van Winkle* as it was originally printed in *The Sketch Book,* which has here been faithfully followed. This edition of *Rip Van Winkle* consists of 1,500 copies made for the members of The Limited Editions Club, with illustrations reproduced from engravings by Felix Darley; printed in Kaatskill type designed and cut for the book by Frederic W. Goudy; set by Bertha M. Goudy at The Village Press, Marlborough-on-Hudson, New York, and printed at the Walpole Printing Office, New Rochelle, New York.

This copy is No.— and is signed by [*F.W. Goudy*].
PAGES: [8] + 57 + [11]. Size 6 x 9¾ inches.

DESIGNS: 6 illustrations by Felix Darley in brown. **1930**
BINDING: Full green leather, title on back in gold. Slip case.

EDITION: 1,500 copies, the 8th volume of The Limited Editions Club. Set by Bertha Goudy in Kaatskill type designed for this book; printed by Walpole Printing Office, New Rochelle, New York. May.

191. Jemima Condict, Her Book

JEMIMA CONDICT | HER BOOK | *Being* | A TRANSCRIPT OF THE DIARY OF | AN ESSEX COUNTY MAID | DURING THE | REVOLUTIONARY | WAR | NEWARK, NEW JERSEY | THE CARTERET BOOK CLUB | MCMXXX

COLOPHON: *Jemima Condict, Her Book* has been made for the Carteret Book Club of Newark, New Jersey, in an edition of 200 copies, by Frederic and Bertha Goudy at The Village Press, Marlborough-on-Hudson, N.Y. It has been set by Mrs. Goudy in 12 point Kaatskill designed by Mr. Goudy, with type cast from matrices cut by them especially for this book. Also the Deepdene Italics were designed by Mr. Goudy. Printed in June, 1930.

PAGES: [10] + 73 + [5]. Size 4½ x 7¼ inches.

DESIGNS: Frontispiece, offset reproduction of diary

1930 page; various other illustrations. Pages ruled throughout in red.

BINDING: Blue boards with all-over pattern of figures in darker blue, white linen back; title in gold on back.

EDITION: 200 copies at $7.50. Set by Bertha Goudy in 12 pt. Kaatskill (cut for this book) and Deepdene Italic; printed by the Walpole Printing Office, New Rochelle, for the Carteret Book Club.

COMMENT: The superior letters used in the text are cast from the smallest matrices Mr. Goudy ever cut.

Fugitive Item

192. A 16th CENTURY CHRISTMAS CARD

Eight-page folder, 4 x 5¾ inches, self cover, sewed with red silk and hand-colored in red. Christmas card containing 3 verses of *Chrystmass Tyme*. Printed on B. F. K. paper in Goudy Text and Mediaeval, its first use. Decorative unit, Christmas tree in tub, by F. W. Goudy.

193. The Song of Songs

1931 THE | SONG | OF | SONGS [*woodcut; title continued on recto following with woodcut*] | WITH WOODCUTS BY | JAMES REID | FARRAR & RINEHART · INC · | ON MURRAY HILL | NEW YORK | 1931

PAGES: [2] + [75 unnumbered] + [3]. Size 7 x 10 inches.

DESIGNS: Numerous woodcuts by James Reid.

BINDING: Blue cloth, title and illustration printed in black on side.

EDITION: 2,000 copies. Set by Bertha Goudy in Newstyle; printed on a gray paper with green tint blocks by the Walpole Printing Office, New Rochelle. October.

Fugitive Items

194. MARKS OF THE EARLY ITALIAN PRINTERS

Eight-page signature, 8½ x 10½ inches, printed in red and black for insertion in *The Colophon*. Reproductions of numerous printers' devices. Set by Bertha Goudy, the first 2 pages in Truesdell, the balance in Mediaeval—the first use of the former and the first considerable appearance of the latter. Printed on Worthy Signature by the Walpole Printing Office, New Rochelle. February.

195. LOUISE ACRES

Leaf, 6 x 9 inches, on Aurelian, containing 16 lines of poetry signed 'W. H. S.' Initial 'W' in Goudy Ornate. About 100 copies.

1931 196. THE GOUDYS WISH YOU ... MERRY CHRISTMAS
Card, 7½ x 5⅝ inches, printed one side in black and hand-colored in red. Row of Christmas trees across top. Set in Trajan capitals. December.

197. THE TYPE SPEAKS
Broadside, 8½ x 11 inches, set in Truesdell Italic, "designed, engraved and composed" by F. W. Goudy. Only a few proofs pulled, never distributed. Dec. 30.

1932 198. EXCERPT, SECOND INAUGURAL ADDRESS
Broadside, 17½ x 23½ inches. Set in Trajan capitals; 160 copies printed on Little Chart.
The line reading 'MARCH 4TH · MDCCCLXV' was first set in 30 pt., but seemed too large. Mr. Goudy thereupon stopped presswork and cut these sorts in 24 pt., substituted this size and resumed printing.
Reprints were made in 1934 and 1936.

199. JOHANN WOLFGANG VON GOETHE
Broadside, 19½ x 14½ inches, printed in black and red. Shows 2 facing pages from a conversation with Johann Peter Eckermann concerning literary style, April 14, 1824. Set in 16 pt. Goethe, a type designed for this contribution and here first used. A 4-line in-

itial 'O' in red by F. W. Goudy. About 50 copies on various stocks: Kelmscott, Little Chart, Maidstone, and Worthy Hand and Arrows; 5 on Japan Vellum.

1932

Designed and printed by Mr. Goudy as The Village Press contribution to the Goethe Centenary Exhibition at Leipzic. One hundred printers throughout the world were asked to participate, a condition being that each printer use an extract from Goethe's writings set in the language of his (the printer's) country.

200. THE VILLAGE PRESS

Card, 3⅜ x 5¾ inches, set by Bertha Goudy in the Goudy Text, Mediaeval and Kennerley; printed elsewhere for Mitchell Kennerley. For use with exhibits at the Vassar College Library, Poughkeepsie, during an exhibition of Village Press books and an address by F. W. Goudy. April 20.

201. THE ROXBURGHE CLUB OF SAN FRANCISCO

Four-page folder, 5½ x 8½ inches, first page only printed in red and black. A 10-line initial 'T' in red by F. W. Goudy. November.

202. AQUA VITAE

Leaf, 8⅝ x 12¼ inches, printed one side in red and black. Christmas card from *Holinshed's Chronicles* of

1932 1577. A 12-line initial 'I,' the same used in the Roxburghe Club invitation (Item No. 201). Set by Bertha Goudy in Trajan, Truesdell and Franciscan; printed for Burgess Johnson on Fabriano by H. W. Coggeshall, Utica, who made some extra copies for Mr. Goudy.

203. GOOD KING WENCESLAS

Eight-page folder, 5½ x 8⅝ inches, printed in red and black. Another Christmas card, reproducing the text of this carol by Dr. Neale which had been printed by The Village Press while in Hingham in 1904 (Item No. 18). Christmas tree and 4-line initial 'G' in red. Set by Bertha Goudy in Village Text (later sold to the Grabhorn Press and renamed Franciscan); printed by Walpole Printing Office. December.

204. Letters

1933 LETTERS | *from T. E. Shaw to Bruce Rogers*

COLOPHON: [On copyright page] 200 copies privately printed at the Press of William Edwin Rudge from type set by Bertha M. Goudy.

PAGES: [6] + [84 *unnumbered*] + [2]. Size 5½ x 8½ inches.

BINDING: Brown cloth over very thin boards. Title in gold on back. Slip case.

EDITION: 200 copies. Set by Bertha Goudy in Deepdene Italic; printed in brown ink by W. E. Rudge, Mount Vernon.

1933

COMMENT: The capitals are 14 pt. cast on 16 pt. body to line with the lowercase, which is the regular 16 pt. Two capitals, the 'N' and T,' are redesigned without swash characteristics. A new set of italic numerals was cut for this book, as well as parentheses and a diagonal. The ampersand is a Linotype sort.

CIRCULAR ROSETTE BY F. W. GOUDY FOR COVER
(ITEM NO. 205)

Fugitive Items

205. SECOND ANNUAL ART EXHIBITION

Sixteen-page pamphlet, 6¼ x 9¼ inches, and cover. Title page, cover and first 3 pages only are Village Press. Set by Bertha Goudy; printed by the Moore Printing Co., Newburgh. April.

1933 206. THE OLD & THE NEW

Twenty-page booklet, 6¼ x 9¾ inches, on Arches, gray (or dark brown) Florentine cover; 230 copies with a 4-line colophon, 70 additional copies with a 3-line added note reading: "This copy is one of 70 printed for presentation to members of the Twelfth Annual Conference on Printing Education on the occasion of their visit to The Village Press, June 25, 1933."

207. GLORIFIER OF THE ALPHABET

Twenty-page pamphlet, 6 x 9 inches, self cover, with an added leaf, *Publisher's Note*. Frontispiece line drawing of F. W. Goudy by William Auerbach-Levy inset against Lincoln broadside (Item No. 198). This and article by Milton Mackaye reprinted (with corrections) from the *New Yorker* for Jan. 14, 1933. Set by Bertha Goudy in Kennerley; printed by the Strathmore Paper Co. and distributed with paper specimen book (Item No. 187) at the Direct Mail Advertising Conference in Chicago. September.

208. THE TYPE SPEAKS

Broadside, 8⅜ x 12½ inches. Text similar to original issue (Item No. 197). Prepared for the Retrospective Exhibition of The Village Press, organized by the

The Type Speaks

❖

I AM TYPE! Of my earliest ancestry neither history nor relics remain. The wedge-shaped symbols impressed in plastic clay by Babylonian builders in the dim past, foreshadowed me: from them, on through the hieroglyphs of the ancient Egyptians, down to the beautiful manuscript letters of the mediaeval scribes, I was in the making.

With the golden vision of the ingenious Gutenberg, who first applied the principle of casting me in metal, the profound art of printing with movable types was born. Cold, rigid, and implacable I may be, yet the first impress of my face brought the Divine Word to countless thousands.

I bring into the light of day the precious stores of knowledge and wisdom long hidden in the grave of ignorance. I coin for you the enchanting tale, the philosopher's moralizing, and the poet's phantasies; I enable you to exchange the irksome hours that come, at times, to every one, for sweet and happy hours with books—golden urns filled with all the manna of the past. In books, I present to you a portion of the eternal mind caught in its progress through the world, stamped in an instant, and preserved for eternity. Through me, Socrates and Plato, Chaucer and the Bards, become your faithful friends who ever surround and minister to you. I am the leaden army that conquers the world; I am Type!

Frederic W. Goudy

1933 American Institute of Graphic Arts to celebrate the 30th anniversary of the Press. A 3-line initial 'T' by F. W. Goudy. Set by Bertha Goudy in Deepdene Italic; printed on a hand-press as a keepsake during the exhibition, Museum of Science and Industry, New York, October 23 to November 19.

Fifteen special copies, 11¼ x 14 inches, printed in red and black on hand-made paper, were also issued.

209. CHRISTMAS BELLS

Four-page folder, 4¾ x 7 inches, in red and black. Holiday greetings in Deepdene Italic and Goudy Text, 4-line initial 'T' in red by F. W. Goudy. December.

210. THE HUDSON-HIGHLANDS ART ASSOCIATION

Four-page folder, 6¼ x 9 inches, in red and black. A 6-line initial 'N' and circular monogram 'H.H.A.A.' by F. W. Goudy.

211. Frankenstein

1934

FRANKENSTEIN | [sketch in green] | OR THE MODERN | PROMETHEUS · BY | MARY WOLLSTONECRAFT SHELLEY | PRINTED WITH AN INTRODUCTION | BY EDMUND LESTER PEARSON AND | ILLUSTRATIONS BY EVERETT HENRY | New York. The Limited Editions Club. Mcmxxxiv

COLOPHON: This edition of *Frankenstein* consists of 1,500 copies printed for the members of The Limited Editions Club at the Walpole Printing Office in New Rochelle, N.Y. The type used is a new design by Frederic W. Goudy, set by hand by Bertha M. Goudy. The illustrations are by Everett Henry who here signs [*signature*].

1934

PAGES: [26] + 257 + [9]. Size 7 x 10¼ inches.

DESIGNS: Various illustrations and initials by Everett Henry.

BINDING: Half morocco, striped linen sides: back gold stamped.

EDITION: 1,500 copies signed by Everett Henry. Set by Bertha Goudy in 14 pt. Goethe, a size cut especially for this work. The Goethe Italic was designed and cut and had its first use in this volume. Printed on Worthy by Walpole Printing Office, New Rochelle. February.

COMMENT: The last book set by Mrs. Goudy.

Fugitive Items

212. TYPOGRAPHICA NO. 6

Sixteen-page pamphlet, 7½ x 10½ inches, blue paper cover. Displays 15 type faces and various fleurons produced by the Village Letter Foundery. Set by Ber-

1934 tha Goudy and George Van Vechten, Jr.; printed by the Mail & Express Printing Co., New York. Prepared for Continental Typefounders Association, Inc. Fall.

213. NATIONAL TEMPLE HILL ASSOCIATION, INC.

Leaf, 14⅜ x 10¼ inches; a membership certificate printed in dark blue ink on Japan Vellum. Set by Bertha Goudy; illustrations by Lee Woodward Ziegler.

214. THE TYPE SPEAKS

Leaf, 8½ x 11 inches. Text as in Item No. 208, but set in Saks-Goudy with 12-line initial 'I.' Subscription says 200 copies were printed at The Village Press in September. Intended for distribution at the Saks Exhibition at the National Arts Club, New York, but not completed in time. Actually first printed, with initial in red and with colophon omitted, in April, 1937.

215. TO MRS. FRANKLIN D. ROOSEVELT

Four-page folder, 8½ x 12 inches, on Tuscany. One copy only, set in Deepdene Italic by Bertha Goudy, printed for Mrs. Russell Kohl and signed by 50 wives of fruit growers in the neighborhood of Marlborough.

216. ARS TYPOGRAPHICA, NUMBER FOUR

Magazine, 52 pages, 8¼ x 12½ inches, gray paper cover printed in red and black. Frontispiece portrait

of William Morris; 3 additional full-page illustrations **1934**
likewise in collotype of F. W. Goudy, Bertha Goudy
and the brook at Deepdene. Various initials by F. W.
Goudy. Each article set in a different Goudy type,
named in the Table of Contents, several being initial
appearances. Set by Bertha Goudy and George Van
Vechten, Jr., at The Village Press; printed on Arak by
the Press of the Woolly Whale, New York; 514 copies
at $2.50 completed in November.

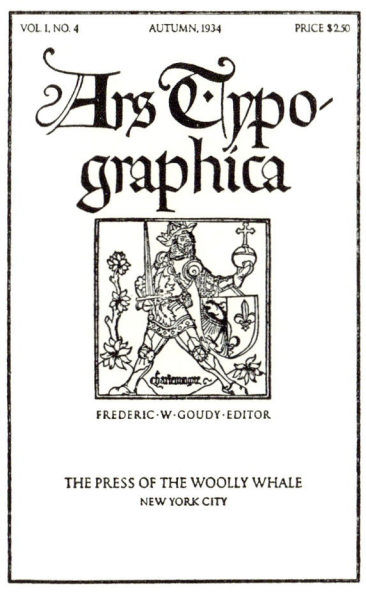

COVER OF "ARS TYPOGRAPHICA," VOLUME I, NUMBER 4

1934 217. FIFTY BOOKS OF THE YEAR

Four-page folder, 7 x 10 inches, printed in brown and black. Call for books for the American Institute of Graphic Arts. A 6-line initial 'T' by F. W. Goudy and device of the Institute in brown. Set at The Village Press by John Archer; printed at the New York Public Library.

218. EXCERPT, SECOND INAUGURAL ADDRESS

Broadside, 17½ x 23½ inches. This second edition is identical with the original (Item No. 198), except that the word 'An' has been added to the first line. Less than 100 copies printed for a meeting of the Typophiles, December 19th.

219. EX LIBRIS, FANNY BORDEN

Bookplate, 1¾ x 2⅜ inches. Monogram 'F.B.' by F. W. Goudy. Set by him as a Christmas gift from her associates to Miss Borden, Librarian of the Vassar College Library, Poughkeepsie, N.Y.

220. A CHRISTMAS GREETING

Four-page folder, 5¾ x 7¼ inches, printed in red and black. Set in the Deepdene Text, with a verse on the third page.

221. THE PENN MUTUAL LIFE INSURANCE CO.   1935

Policy, 5 sheets 8½ x 14 inches, in black and brown. Set by Frederic Truesdell Goudy in Mediaeval, Village No. 2 and Deepdene; printed by the Company.

222. TO MR. AND MRS. VERMONT HATCH

Broadside, 20 x 26 inches. A testimonial "from the craftsmen who have participated in the erection of this building" to "the man who made it possible for us to find profitable employment during the severest years of the great depression." Set by F. W. and F. T. Goudy in Trajan in one afternoon; one copy. July.

223. RETROSPECTUS

Eight-page insert, 5¾ x 8¾ inches, in red and black, prepared for inclusion in *Barnacles from Many Bottoms,* a tribute to Bruce Rogers issued by the Typophiles. A 7-line initial 'O' in red by F. W. Goudy. Set in 14 pt. Newstyle, cut especially for this insert and dedicated to Bruce Rogers. Composed in part by Bertha Goudy, "the only composition by her since her illness, in order that she, too, might have some part in this tribute to her dear friend, B. R." This was Mrs. Goudy's last work at the Press. Printed by the Moore Printing Co., Newburgh. August.

1935 224. 1869 · BERTHA M. GOUDY · 1935
Card, 5¾ x 3⅜ inches, announcing the death of Bertha M. Goudy, October 21. Deepdene Italic and Goudy Text.

225. AN ACKNOWLEDGEMENT
Four-page folder, 4½ x 6¼ inches. Acknowledgement of condolences on the occasion of the death of Bertha M. Goudy. Mediaeval. November.

1936 226. EXCERPT, SECOND INAUGURAL ADDRESS
Broadside, 17½ x 23½ inches. This third edition is identical with the second (Item No. 218), except that the fleuron used between the 4th and 5th lines of the first 2 editions, a cross with diamond-shaped points, is replaced by a star in outline.

227. THIS TREE WAS PRESENTED...
Sixteen-line inscription, 10 x 13 inches, set in Trajan capitals by F. T. Goudy, to be used in conjunction with a sculptured figure by Faggi to form a memorial tablet in memory of John A. Kingsbury, Jr., an Andover student who died in an automobile accident. The only type impressions were a few proofs. A plaster cast made from the type form was used as a model for the bronze lettering.

228. ANDS AND AMPERSANDS 1936
Fifty-eight-page insert, 4 x 6⅛ inches, in red and black, prepared for inclusion in *Diggings from Many Ampersandhogs*, a Christmas volume prepared by the Typophiles. More than 65 forms of the ampersand, for which drawings were made and matrices cut by F.W. Goudy, are illustrated. Originally set by F. T. Goudy in Bertham; reset in Deepdene and printed by H.W. Coggeshall, Utica, N.Y.
About 100 copies separately bound in gray paper.

229. THE MEDAL OF HONOR
Four-page folder, 6 x 9 inches, in red and black. Invitation to a dinner given by the Ulster-Irish Society of New York, March 19th, when its Medal of Honor was conferred on F.W. Goudy "for distinguished service to the graphic arts." Set by F.T. Goudy in Village No. 2; printed at the New York Public Library. 1937

230. THE ULSTER-IRISH SOCIETY OF NEW YORK
Four-page folder, 7⅜ x 10⅝ inches, in red and black. Keepsake written by Earl Emmons and set by him at The Village Press in Tory, the first use of this type. Largely reset by F. W. and F. T. Goudy to accommodate a 9-line initial 'W' in red by F.W. Goudy. Printed

·The Ulster-Irish Society of New York·
On the Occasion of Presentation of its Fifth Medal to
Frederic W. Goudy
WHOSE CREATIONS IN TYPOGRAPHIC DESIGN
WILL ENDURE FOREVER

We who are gathered here on this occasion to honor Frederic W. Goudy do well indeed in honoring one who has himself brought such great honor to the craft he serves and so much benefit to all humanity. Goudy once described himself as «just an humble designer of type»; yet this humble type designer has made a record of achievement never before approached, nor is it likely that the achievement ever will be equalled, and in the doing he has exerted a greater influence in graphic art than any other figure in the history of printing. ¶ Stanley Morison of England has said of him, «The types he has designed have had the miraculous effect of transforming the advertising pages of every magazine in America, and a few in our own country.» ¶ Mitchell Kennerley has said, «Goudy has never designed a freak type nor an inferior type. And never in his life has he ever done a single thing that was not one hundred per cent. the best he was able to do.» ¶ Howard Coggeshall calls him «the most renowned creator of printing type we have known, or will know; the most prolific and resourceful contributor to typographic beauty and utility who has ever lived.» ¶ John Clyde Oswald has declared «Of all of those who are identified with printing today the name of Goudy is the only one that will be generally remembered one hundred years from now.» ¶ Indeed the entire civilized world owes a great debt to Goudy. With his more than one hundred type designs and with his tremendous influence upon all others in his craft he has made on a special Worthy Permanent Book carrying a full-page watermark portrait of Mr. Goudy, by the Walpole Printing Office, Mount Vernon. March 19. (See illustration opposite).

1937

231. THE TYPE SPEAKS

Leaf, 7⅞ x 11⅞ inches, intended for Saks Exhibition, 1934 (see Item No. 214). Printed one side in red, but without colophon and with addition of author's name at top, by H. W. Coggeshall, Utica, N. Y. April.

232. THE TYPE SPEAKS

Broadside, 13¼ x 19 inches, set in 18 pt. Trajan capitals. Text slightly altered from previous editions (see Items Nos. 197, 208, 214 and 231). Printed for distribution at the Typophile Christmas gathering, December.

Although this bibliography closes with the year 1937, The Village Press continues. Space to record its further publications is afforded by the following blank pages.

A Bibliography of The Village Press

A Bibliography of The Village Press

An Index to the Bibliography
1903-1938

A 16th Century Christmas Card
    Item 192   172
Acres, Dr. Louise, 76, 124, 170, 173
Address to the Graduating Class
    Item 68   102
Adler, Elmer, 140
Advertisement of the Village Press, 39
    Item 8   55
    Item 63   98
Albion Press
    From Caslon & Co., 26, 121
    From William Morris, 153, 154, 155, 158, 159, 160, 161
    Illustrated 157
Alphabet, The, 97, 146, 150
    Item 132   132
    Illustrated 133
American Cat News, 47
American Institute of Graphic Arts, 121, 127, 139, 140, 145, 150, 151, 180, 184
    Item 98   119
    Item 156   145
    Item 166   151
American Printer, The, 144, 151, 154
American Printers' Series, 155, 159
American Type Founders Co., 10, 36
American's Creed, The, 142
An Acknowledgement
    Item 225   186
An Appreciation: Elmer Adler
    Item 142   140

Anderson Galleries, 155, 157, 159, 160, 161
Ands and Ampersands
    Item 228   187
Announcement Concerning Summer Reading
    Item 109   122
Announcement by Mr. Laurence J. Gomme
    Item 100   120
Announcement of Ivan Somerville & Co.
    Item 62   97
Announcements of The Village Press, 39
    No. 1   54
    No. 2   55
    No. 3   55
    No. 4   56
    No. 5   56
    No. 6   59
    No. 7   64
    No. 8   72
    No. 9   77
    No. 10   78
    Illustrated 78
    No. 11   86
Annual Report, Lanston Monotype
    Item 163   150
Aqua Vitae
    Item 202   175
Archer, John, 184
Architectural Sketch Club, 9
Areopagitica: A Speech for the Liberty of Un-licensed Printing, 110
Argument for . . . A National Weekly, An
    Item 79   110

An Index to the Bibliography

Ars Typographica, 47, 117, 121, 142, 146, 164
   No. 1, Item 134   134
         Illustrated 135
   No. 2, Item 135   136
         Illustrated 136
   No. 3, Item 147   142
   No. 4, Item 216   182
         Illustrated 183
Art and the Great War
   Item 138   137
Art Director for the Monotype, An
   Item 149   144
Art in Type Design, 168
Art Institute, Chicago, 18, 33, 34
Art Typography, 143
Arts & Crafts Essays, 51
Arts & Crafts Society, 62
Ashendene Press, 45
At The Fireside
   Item 26   70
Auerbach-Levy, William, 178
Baldwin, Prof. Samuel A., 124, 125, 162
Bancroft, Edgar, 53
Banning, Hedwig, 76
Banning, Kendall, 76, 80, 108
Barnacles from Many Bottoms, 185
Barnard, Charles H., 107, 111, 112
Barnard's Monographs On Design, 94
   Item 83   111
Bartlett, Alfred, 70, 71, 94
Bassette Co., F. A., 139
Batchelor & Sons, 29
Beardsley, Aubrey, 14
Beauley, William Jean, 16
Beck Engraving Co., 137
Bell, R. Anning, 94, 96
Bianco, Miss Pamela, 144
Beilenson, Peter, 165
Bertha M. Goudy, 1869-1935
   Item 224   186

Bird, Elisha Brown, 71, 81
Bird, Jack, 35, 36
Birmingham (England) Guild of Handicraft, 66
Birrell, Augustine, 155, 158
Blessed Damozel, The, 29, 31, 59
   Item 3   53
Blind Princess & the Dawn, The
   Item 14   58
Book Beautiful, The
   See: Extracts from
Book-Binding, 158
Book-Buying, 158
Book for a Wedding, A
   Item 2   52
Book of Portraits, A
   Item 160   149
Book of Signatures, A
   Item 172   162
Book Plates of Elisha B. Bird
   Item 42   81
Booklet Press, The, 8, 46, 146
Books: The Art of the Book, 109
Books as Doctors
   Item 112   124
Books for Sale & in Preparation
   Item 10   55
   Item 11   56
   Item 12   56
   Item 49   86
Books Not Dead Things
   Item 81   110
Borden, Miss Fanny, 6, 184
Bowdoin, W. G., 77, 87
Bowles, J. M., 87
Bowling Green Press, 167, 168
Branca, Frank, 148
Brentano's Book Stores, Inc., 129
British Museum, 23
Brothers of the Book, 108
Browning, Robert, 62

An Index to the Bibliography

Bruere, Robert, 62, 69
Bunch of Violets, The
    Item 52   87
Burne-Jones, 159
Caduceus, illustrated, 118
Calkins, Ernest Elmo, 14
Camelot Press, The, 8, 9, 11, 12, 13, 46
Carman, Bliss, 14, 15, 75, 85, 86, 88, 90, 100, 102
Carteret Book Club, 171, 172
Cary, Melbert B., Jr., 45, 156
Cascade at Deepdene, The, 166
Case, Elizabeth York, 83, 84
Caslon, H. W. & Co., 119, 120, 121
Caxton, 6, 66
Cedar Rapids Savings Bank, 36
Chambers, J., 80
Chap Book, The, 8, 13, 14
Chaucer, 155, 156, 159
Christmas Bells
    Item 209   180
Christmas Carol, A
    Item 46   84
Christmas Carroll, A Poem, A
    Item 113   124
Christmas Greeting, A
    Item 220   184
Christmas, MCMXXIX
    Item 189   170
Chrystmass Tyme, 172
Church of St. John the Evangelist, Lent, 1905
    Item 32   72
City & Country Homes
    Item 55   88
Cobden-Sanderson, 23, 55, 86
Coburn, Alvin Langdon, 103, 105
Cockerell, Sydney, 23
Coffin, Haskell, 139
Coggeshall, H. W., 176, 187, 189
Coleman, McAllister, 140

College of the City of New York, 125, 162
Colliers' Magazine, 149
Colophon, The, 173
Columbia University, 138
Comment on Kennerley Type
    Item 124   129
Commonwealth Press, 122
Communication from the President, A
    Item 157   145
Compliments of the Season, The
    Item 181   166
Condict, Jemima, Her Book
    Item 191   171
Condit, Sarah Emily, In Memoriam
    Item 50   87
Conference on Printing Education, 178
Confessio Amantis, A Sonnet, 169
    Item 126   129
Continental Typefounders Association, Inc., 165, 166, 182
Cooper, Fred, 131
Cooper, Oswald, 33
Copeland & Day, 14
Cornish Brothers, 63
Cosgrave, J. O'Hara, 110
Craftsman's Ideal, The
    Item 152   144
Crane & Co., 141
Currier, Everett, 90
Currier Press, 151
Darley, Felix, 170, 171
de Colonia, John, 109, 111
de Forest, Dr. Lee, 93
Dean, Eva, 90
Declaration, In the Name of God, Amen, A
    Item 130   131
Deepdene
    Marlborough, 19, 164, 166
    Type, 165, 166, 169
        Illustrated, 166

An Index to the Bibliography

Deepdene: A New Type
    Item 179   165
    Illustrated 166
Deserted Village, The, 39
Destruction of The Village Press by Fire, The, 89
Dial, The, 55
Diary of Will Ransom, 33
Dickens Centenary Fund, 113
Dickinson Type Foundry, 10
Diehl, Edith, 113, 148
Diggings from Many Ampersandhogs, 187
Dignity
    Item 141   139
Dillon, Robert, 9
Dinner of the Stowaways, A
    Item 85   112
Diploma of the Unitrinian School
    Item 74   107
Direct Mail Advertising Conference, 178
Dissertation Upon Roast Pig, A, 39, 59
    Item 13   56
Door in the Wall, The
    Item 70   103, 104
    Illustrated 105
Doves Press, 24
    Type   21
Drinkwater, John, 167
Duckworth & Co., 158
Duschnes, Philip C., 20
Dutton & Co., E. P., 137
Dwiggins, W. A., 62, 63
Ebb Tide, The, 14
Eckermann, Johann Peter, 174
1896 · Bertha M. Goudy · 1935
    Item 224   186
Elements of Lettering, 150
    Item 158   146
    Illustrated 147
Eliot, Dr. Charles William, 65, 96

Emerson as Seer, 64, 65, 72
    Item 60   96
Emmons, Earl H., 44, 187
Encyclopedia Britannica, 109
Enright, Walter J., 67
Essays of Elia, 56
Ex Libris, Fanny Borden
    Item 219   184
Excerpt, Second Inaugural Address
    Item 198   174
    Item 218   184
    Item 226   186
Exhibition, An
    Item 84   111
Exhibition of American Printing, 127
    Item 118   126
Exhibition of Old Masters
    Item 89   113
Exhibition of Pictorial Photographs
    Item 137   136
Extracts from The Book Beautiful
    Item 48   86
Extracts from the Diary of Will Ransom, 33
Facsimile Trial Pages: Froissart's Chronicles
    Item 145   141
Faculty, College of Physicians & Surgeons
    Item 139   138
Faggi, 186
Fairbanks, Thomas Nast, 109
Faith & Reason
    Item 45   84
Farningham, Unbleached Arnold
    Item 120   128
Farquhar, James D., 3
Farrar & Rinehart, Inc., 172
Fay, Charles, 11
Field, Eugene, 5, 19
Field, Marshall, 11
Field, Roswell, 19, 20
Fifty Books of the Year
    Item 217   184

An Index to the Bibliography

First Christmas Tree, The
    Item 76   107
First Days of the Village Press, The, 33
First Goudy Christmas Card, The
    Item 93   117
Flatbush, 98
Florence Hotel, 93
Foley, P. K., 73
Ford, Julia Ellsworth, 97
Forefathers' Day, 86, 88
    Item 59   96
Forest Hills Gardens, N. Y., 117-151
    Residence and Press Illustrated, 116
Forest Hills Gardens Bulletin
    Item 148   143
Forest Hills Gardens: Fourth Annual Celebration
    Item 131   131
Forest Trees, The
    Item 92   115
Forum Type, 119, 120
    First Received, 98
Four Poems
    Item 33   72
Four Poems by James Russell Lowell
    Item 34   73
Franciscan type, 176
Frankenstein, 181
    Item 211   180
Franklin, Benjamin, 151
Fred W. Goudy and Will H. Ransom
    Item 4   54
Frederic & Bertha Goudy, Announcement
    Item 39   78
Friendship, An Essay
    Item 121   128
Froissart's Chronicles, 135, 141, 155
Gage, Lyman, 11
Gallatin, Albert Eugene, 137
Garland, Hamlin, 14

Gaskin, Arthur, 63
Gate of Peace, The, 88, 90
    Item 47   85
Gate of Peace, The, A Poem
    Item 57   89
Genthe, Arnold, 117, 157
Germ, The, 53, 54
Gettysburg Address, The
    Item 119   127
    Illustrated 127
Gilliss, Walter, 145
Gimbel & Co., 128
Glorifier of the Alphabet
    Item 207   178
Goerke, Frank S., 148
Goethe Centenary Exhibition, 175
Goethe, Johann Wolfgang von
    Item 199   174
Golden Legend, 66
Golden type, 10, 17, 21
Golding Press, 100, 101, 102
Gomme, Laurence J., 120, 121, 122, 123, 124, 126
Good Bishop Valentine
    Item 87   112
Good King Wenceslas
    Item 18   63
    Item 203   176
Good News to Forest Hills Gardens
    Item 122   128
Goodhue, Bertram G., 15, 21
Goodlye Doctrine & Instruction
    Item 127   130
Gorham, Edwin S., 107
Goudy Antique type, 110
Goudy, Bertha M. (Sprinks), 16, 29, 30, 31, 37, 38, 40, 41, 47, 76, 98, 124, 125, 134, 161, 162, 181, 185, 186
    Illustration, 44
Goudy, Frederic Truesdell, 90, 185, 187

An Index to the Bibliography

Goudy, Frederic William, 54, 69, 83, 98, 111, 119, 121, 135, 144, 145, 150, 151, 165, 178, 187
    Introduction by, 1-32
    Parker Building fire, 89-93
    Note on the Albion Press, 153-158
    Photograph, opposite Page 1
    Photograph with Morris Press, 157
    Watermark portrait, 189
Goudy Lanston type, 108, 110
Goudy Modern type
    First showing, 136
Goudys Wish You, The
    Item 196   174
Grabhorn Press, 176
Grand Central Palace, 118
Graphic Arts, 88
Graphic Arts Exposition, 165, 166
Greene, Belle Da Costa, 112
Gress, Edmund G., 151, 154
Grolier Club, 155, 158, 159
Grolier, Jean, An Excerpt
    Item 104   121
Guild of Book-Workers, The
    Item 54   88
Gunsaulus, Dr. Frank, 4
Gutenberg's Invention
    Item 188   169
Guthrie, James, 154
Gypsy Trail, The
    Item 27   70
    Item 28   71
Hadriano type
    First showing, 135
Hallock, Ruth Mary, 79
Hand-Press Printing: A Plea for a Lost Craft, 142
Hapgood, T. B., 14
Hart, Schaffner & Marx, 16
Hatch, Mr. & Mrs. Vermont, 185
Heine, Heinrich
    Item 69   103

Hellmuth ink, 38
Henry, Everett, 180, 181
Higginbotham, Thomas, 11
Hingham Glee Club, The
    Item 31   72
Hingham, Mass., 61-73
    Residence and Press Illustrated, 60
Hingham Society of Arts & Crafts
    Item 19   64
Hippocrates, The Oath of
    Item 115   125
Hoeber, Paul B., 125, 130, 138
Hoggson Bros., 88
Holinshed's Chronicles, 175
Hollow Land, The, 29, 32, 41, 56, 69
    Item 25   67
    Illustrated 68
Holme, Frank, 16
    School of Illustration, 33
Honorary President of the A.I.G.A.
    Item 165   151
Hooper, Cyrus Lauron, 7, 8, 11, 56, 57, 67, 69, 146
Hornby, St. John, 23, 46
Horter, Earl, 115
Hovey, Richard, 14
Hudson-Fulton Celebration, 89
Hudson-Highlands Art Association, The
    Item 210   180
Hughes, Thomas C., 148
Hungerford, Edward, 115
Hunter, George Leland, 11
Ideal Book, The, 24, 39
    Item 9   55
If I were Pan, 102
Illian, George, 148, 149
Important Announcement to Printers
    Item 176   164
In Memoriam Sarah Emily Condit
    Item 50   87

An Index to the Bibliography

In the Wake of the Stowaways
    Item 155   145
Independence Day Proclamation, 141
Ink, 24, 25, 26, 38, 39, 40
Inland Printer, 15
Interior Decoration, 94, 98
    Item 53   87
International Typographic Council
    Item 180   166
Interpretative Photography
    Item 86   112
Irving, Washington, 109, 170
Italian Hand-Made Paper
    Item 71   106
Jack and Jill
    Item 37   77
Jaeger, Doris U., 138
    See also: Ulmann, Doris
Jaenecke ink, 24, 39, 40
Japan Paper Co., 28, 128
Jean Grolier: An Excerpt
    Item 104   121
Jemima Condict, Her Book
    Item 191   171
Jenson type, 10
Johann Wolfgang von Goethe
    Item 199   174
John A. Staples Wishes You . . .
    Item 174   164
Johns Hopkins University Press, 149
Johnson, Burgess, 176
Johnson, Henry Lewis, 88
Jordan, Wm., 80
Keepsake, 151, 159, 160, 166, 187
Kellogg, Spencer, 158
Kelmscott Press, 7, 10, 23, 45, 134, 155, 156, 158, 159
Kennerley type, 89, 98, 104, 120, 129
Kennerley, Mitchell, 82, 103, 117, 121, 132, 133, 134, 146, 175

Kidd: A Moral Opuscule
    Item 159   148
Kimball, Ingalls, 8, 13
King, Mary Perry, 102
Kingsbury, John A., Jr., 186
Kipling, Rudyard, 70, 71
Knickerbocker, Diedrich, 170
Kohl, Mrs. Russell, 182
Kuppenheimer & Co., 16, 17, 18
La Barre, O. H., 103
Lady of Shalott, The, 8
Lamb, Charles, 56
Lambert, Dr. Samuel W., 138
Lamb's Literary Motive, 56
Lane, John, 82
Lanston Monotype Machine Co., 128, 144, 161, 168
Lark Ascending, The
    Item 171   161
Laurence J. Gomme Visited The Village Press
    Item 116   126
Lawrence Publishing Co., 15
Le Bonheur de ce Monde, 142
LeGallienne, Richard, 112, 123, 124
Lee, Georgia M., 79
Lent 1905, Church of St. John the Evangelist
    Item 32   72
Letter Design
    See: Notes on Letter Design
Letters
    Item 204   176
Letters & Lettering, 34
Library of Congress, 82
Limited Editions Club, 170, 171, 180, 181
Lincoln, Abraham, 174, 178, 184, 186
Linn, John Weber, 59
Linotype, 177
List of the Books For Sale and in Preparation
    Item 29   72

An Index to the Bibliography

Little Book Shop Around The Corner, The, 121, 122
    Item 88   113
Little Girl and her Doll, The, 77
Little Meeting, Farmington, Conn., 128
London Magazine, 56
Long, John D., 70
Louise Acres
    Item 195   173
Louisiana Purchase Exposition, Village Press books exhibited
    Item 1   52
    Item 3   54
    Item 13   58
    Item 25   69
Love and Life, 108
Lover's Hours, The
    Item 43   82
Lowell, James Russell, 72, 73, 88, 96
Luther, Agnes Vinton, 87
Lyf of Seynt Kenelme Kynge and Martir
    Item 24   66
Mackaye, Milton, 178
Mail & Express Printing Co., 182
Marchbanks Press, 126, 130, 131, 135, 136, 138, 141, 142, 143, 144, 145, 146, 150
    Press mark, illustrated, 143
Marder, Clarence C., 31, 39, 53
Marder, Luse & Co., 15
Marks of the Early Italian Printers
    Item 194   173
Marlborough, N.Y., 152-189
    Exterior of the Mill, Frontispiece
    Interior of the Mill, 152
Marshall Field & Co., 16
Massachusetts
    Item 23   65
Maverick Press, 100
McClurg, A. C. & Co., 4, 6, 7, 16, 20, 32, 33
McMurtrie, Douglas C., 164, 165

McVickar, Henry Goelet, 101
Medal of Honor, The
    Item 229   187
Men, Women & Books, 158
Meredith, George, 161
Mergenthaler Linotype Co., 177
Merrymount type, 17, 21
Meteyard, Tom, 14
Metropolitan Insurance Tower, 93
Michigan Farmer, 15
Mill, The Old, frontispiece
    Interior, 152
Millard, George, 5, 7, 32
Millay, Edna St. Vincent, 155
Milton, John, 110
Mirabeau's Tribute to Benjamin Franklin
    Item 164   151
Modern Advertising, 47
Monahan, Michael, 103
Monograms of The Village Press
    First (3rd press mark),
        Illustrated, 57
    Second (4th press mark),
        Illustrated, 100
Monotype
    See: Lanston Monotype Co.
Monotype, Goudy Number
    Item 184   168
Montaigne type, 17, 21
Montross Art Galleries, 111
Moore, James, 36
Moore Printing Co., 177, 185
Morningside Park, 90
Morris, Frank, 4
Morris, William, 7, 10, 17, 19, 20, 21, 23, 29, 31, 32, 45, 51, 63, 64, 67, 135, 141, 153, 154, 155, 156, 158, 159, 160, 183
Morris Press
    See: Albion Press
Mr. & Mrs. F. W. Goudy Cordially Invite
    Item 170   161

An Index to the Bibliography

Munder, N. T. A., 101, 104, 106, 107, 119, 123, 150
Museum of Science & Industry, 180
Music, 162
   Item 114   124
Nadal, Bernard, 12, 15
National Arts Club, 139, 140, 182
National Child Welfare Association, Inc., 130
National Cloak & Suit Co., 114
National Printing and Advertising Exposition, 118
National Temple Hill Association, Inc.
   Item 213   182
Neale, Dr. John Mason, 63, 176
New Connection, A
   Item 103   120
New-Year Civilities
   Item 78   109
New York, 74-115
New York Metropolitan Museum of Art, 89
New York Public Library, 184, 187
New Yorker, 178
Newberry Library, 7
News from the Printers' Paradise
   Item 162   150
Newstyle type
   First showing, 144
Next Meeting of the Stowaways, The
   Item 51   87
Nine Poems
   Item 94   117
Ninety-First Psalm, The
   Item 16   61
Nonne Preestes Tale, The, 72
Nordfeldt, Bror. J. Olsson, 67, 69
Note on Letter-Design & the Village Types, A
   Item 110   122
   Illustrated 123
Note on the Village Press & Type, A
   Item 6   55

Notes on Letter Design
   Item 56   88
Notice to . . . Buyers of the Village Press Books
   Item 38   77
Novel Type Foundry, A
   Item 96   118
   Caduceus illustrated, 118
   Item 97   119
Now Ready, Kennerley . . . Forum Title
   Item 102   120
Oath of Hippocrates, The
   Item 115   125
Obiter Dicta, 158
Office of Literature, The, 158
Old & the New, The
   Item 206   178
Old Stratford Book Papers
   Item 187   169
Open Letter from Richard LeGallienne, An, 124
   Item 111   123
Order Blank for Printing, 38, 55
Our Alphabet, A Handbook of Letters, 97
Our Noble Art, 122
Oxford & Cambridge Magazine, 32, 67
Page Designs from Modern American Books, 108
Page, Wm. Tyler, 142
Painter's Holiday, A
   Item 66   100
Parable of the Wise and Foolish Young Men
   Item 123   129
Park Ridge, Ill., 19, 36, 50-59, 64, 69
   Location of Press, Illustrated, 50
Parker Building, 58, 64, 65, 82, 86, 89, 90, 92, 93, 94, 96, 97
   Illustrated, 74
Paton, Sir Noel, 84
Pearson, Edmund Lester, 180
Penn Mutual Life Insurance Co., The
   Item 221   185
Perfect Woman, The
   Item 36   76

An Index to the Bibliography

Perkins, Frances, 19
Personal Message, A
 Item 128 130
Peters, Paul J., 148
Philobiblon: A Ricardo de Bury Scriptum
 Item 151 144
 Item 154 145
Pionola Recital Season
 Item 90 113
  Illustrated 114
Picciola, 3
Pictorial Photographers of America, 112
Piers Ploughman, 3
Place Cards
 Item 150 144
Plantin, Christoph, 117, 142
Pocono Building, 91
Poems of Sir John Suckling, 5
Pollard, Alfred, 15
Pollard, Percival, 14
Pont, Charles E., 152
Portrait Gallery, A
 Item 173 163
Potter, Louis, 130
Press (machine)
 See: Albion
   Golding
   Schneidewend & Lee
   Thomson, John
   Washington
Press of the Woolly Whale, 17, 156, 183
Press Marks—The Village Press
  (all illustrated)
 1st press mark, 49
 2nd press mark, 54
 3rd (1st Monogram), 57
 4th (2nd Monogram), 100
  First use, item 73, 107
 5th press mark, 109
  First use, item 82, 111
Prince, Edward, 23
Princess of the Tower, The, 89
 Item 35 75

Printing, 19, 27, 31, 36, 38, 39, 40, 55, 56
 Item 1 51
Printing Art, The, 39
Printing Art at the National Exposition, The
 Item 95 118
Printing Exhibition, May 5 to June 1
 Item 143 140
Printing House of William Edwin Rudge
 See: Rudge
Private Presses & their Books, 20
Proclamation, By the President to the People, A
 Item 129 131
Procter, Robert, 23
Promotheus, The Modern, 180
Prospectus for
 The Alphabet
  Item 136 136
 Barnard's Monographs
  Item 75 107
 The Door in the Wall
  Item 72 106
 Elements of Lettering
  Item 161 150
Publisher's Note, 178
Publishers Printing Co., 117, 120
Quest, The, 66
Quinn, John, 117
Rabbi Ben Ezra
 Item 17 62
Ransom, Will, 18, 19, 20, 27, 30, 33, 56, 154
Reed, Philip G., 50
Reid, James, 172, 173
Removal Announcement
 Item 21 64
Renascence, 155
 Item 169 161
Retrospective Exhibition of The Village Press, 178
Retrospectus
 Item 223 185

An Index to the Bibliography

Ricketts, Charles, 6
Rip Van Winkle
   Item 190   170
Riverside Press, 99
Rogers & Company, 118
Rogers, Bruce, 15, 21, 98, 99, 148, 149, 176, 185
Rosenbaum, S. G., An Appreciation
   Item 91   114
Rossetti, Dante Gabriel, 53
Roxburghe Club of San Francisco, The, 176
   Item 201   175
Ruckstuhl, C. E., 126, 129
Rudge, William Edwin, 128, 132, 134, 136, 137, 140, 141, 142, 148, 149, 150, 163, 167, 168, 176, 177
Russell, Sol Smith, 5
Ruzicka, Rudolph, 65, 96
Saint Matthew, Gospel According to, 94
Saints' and Sinners' Corner, 4
Saks Exhibition, 182, 189
Saks-Goudy type, 182
Salmagundi, 109
Schmidt, Charles P., Jr., 77
Schneidewend & Lee Press, 24, 154
School of Illustration, Chicago, 16
Scott, Temple, 111
Scotto, Ottaviano, 111
Scribner's Sons, Charles, 97, 158
Season's Greetings, The
   Item 185   168
Second Annual Art Exhibition
   Item 205   177
   Illustrated 177
Sermon in the Mount, The, 86, 88
   Item 58   94
   Illustrated 95
Sharp, William, 14
Shaw, Oscar, 92
Shaw, T. E., 176

Shelley, Mary Wollstonecraft, 180
Sherman, Frederic F., 97, 100
Sherman type, 101
Shipman, Louis Evan, 163
Shipping Label
   Item 105   121
Simeon Solomon
   Item 61   97
16th Century Christmas Card, A
   Item 192   172
Sketch Book, The, 170
Smith, Charles W., frontispiece
Society of Printers, Boston, 129
Some Thoughts on the Ornamented MSS. of the Middle Ages, 156
Somerville & Co., Ivan, 83, 84, 85, 97
Song of Songs, The
   Item 140   138
   Item 193   172
Songs and Verses, 86, 88
   Item 65   99
Songs for a Wedding Day, 86, 98
   Item 41   80
Specimen of Types, A
   Item 153   145
Songs of the Love Unending, 110
   Item 77   108
Staples, John A., 164
Starr, Miss Frances, 139
Steinway Art Cases
   Item 101   120
Stevenson, Robert L., 14
Stone & Kimball, 8, 13, 14
Stone, Herbert, 13
Stone, Melville, 13
Stone, Wilbur Macy, 80
Story of the Village Type, The, 17
Stowaways, The, 87, 112, 122, 145, 161
   Item 80   110
Strathmore Paper Co., 139, 169, 178
Strode, William, 124

An Index to the Bibliography

Stryker, Dr., 5
Subiaco type, 23
Subscription Blank
    Item 30   72
Summer Reading, Announcement Concerning
    Item 109   122
Supplement to Typographica No. 3
    Item 125   129
Tabard Press, The, 102, 110
Taylor & Taylor, 126
Tennyson, Alfred Lord, 8
There is no Unbelief
    Item 44   83
This Keepsake is the First Impression
    Item 168   159
    Illustrated 160
This Tree was Presented . . .
    Item 227   186
Thomas, Theodore, 11
Thomsen-Ellis Co., 151
Thomson Press, John, 142
Three Essays, 155
    Item 167   158
To Mr. and Mrs. Vermont Hatch
    Item 222   185
To Mrs. Franklin D. Roosevelt
    Item 215   182
To the Graphic Group
    Item 106   121
To the Residents of Forest Hills Gardens
    Item 146   141
To the Stowaways, An Invitation
    Item 108   122
To the Trade, 39
To The Village Press, 38
    Item 5   55
To the Winged Victory, 75
Tommy and Betty
    Item 40   79
Tory type
    First use   187
    Illustrated 188

Towne, Charles Hanson, 167
Trial Impression of Deepdene Italic
    Item 186   169
Tribune, Chicago, 11
Tribute to our Fallen Aviators, A
    Item 133   134
Triptych, The, 80
True Amazing Story of the Invention of Printing, 169
Truesdell, Winfred Porter, 81
Twelfth Annual Conference on Printing Education, 178
Twilight Park, 102
Two Singers
    Item 182   167
Type faces
    See under individual names
Type Speaks, The
    Item 197   174
    Item 208   178
        Illustrated 179
    Item 214   182
    Item 231   189
    Item 232   189
Typographica
    No. 1
        Item 73   106
    No. 2
        Item 82   111
    No. 3
        Item 117   126
    No. 3 Supplement
        Item 125   129
    No. 4
        Item 175   164
    No. 5
        Item 177   165
    No. 6
        Item 212   181
Typologia, 144
Typophiles, 184, 185, 187, 189
Ulmann, Doris, 149, 163
    See also: Jaeger, Doris U.

An Index to the Bibliography

Ulster-Irish Society of New York, The, 19
    Item 230   187
        Illustrated 188
Undine, 3
University of California Medical School, 126
Updike, D. B., 15, 66
Vale Press, 5, 6
Valuable Documents—Crane's
    Item 144   141
Van Doren, Mark, 170
Van Vechten, George, Jr., 182, 183
Vassar College Library, 6, 83, 175, 184
Vathek, 3
Verses, by McVickar
    Item 67   101
Viatores Tres Itinere
    Item 7   55
Vicar of Wakefield, 3
Victor Electric Co., 131
Village Blacksmith, The, 19
Village Letter Foundery, 106, 164, 165, 181
Village Press, The
    Item 200   175
    Beginnings, by F. W. Goudy, 1-32
    Beginnings, by Will Ransom, 33-41
    Publications, 1903-1904, 51-59
    Publications, 1904-1906, 61-73
    Publications, 1906-1913, 75-115
    Destruction by Fire, 89-93
    Publications, 1913-1923, 117-151
    Publications, 1923-1937, 153-189
Village Press Publications, The
    Item 15   59
Village type, 20, 21, 23, 91
Village Types, The
    Item 99   119
Walker, Sir Emery, 15, 22, 23, 51, 156
Walker Engraving Co., The, 132

Waller, Edmund, 88, 99
Walpole Printing Office, 165, 170, 171, 172, 173, 176, 181, 189
Walpole Society, 99
Walpole's Friends in Boston, Mr., 98
    Item 64   99
Walsh, Richard J., 148, 149
Warren, Waldo P., 16
Washington hand press, 26
Watermark portrait of Mr. Goudy, 189
Watts, George F., 53, 80, 108
Way, W. Irving, 5, 13, 33
Weber, Max, 112
Weinstock, Henry M., 16, 17
Wells, H. G., 103, 105
Whale
    See: Press of the Woolly Whale.
White, Clarence H., 151
White, L. F., Co., 165
White, Marian Strong, 128
Why We Have Chosen Forest Hills
    Item 107   122
Wiebking, Robert, 22, 23, 35, 38, 69, 92, 98, 104
Wilson, Francis, 4
Wise Men from the East, The, 75
Woman's Home Companion, The, 166
Woolly Whale
    See: Press of the Woolly Whale
Work of Frederic W. Goudy,
    Printer & Craftsman, The, 111
World's Lincoln, The, 169
    Item 183   167
Worthy Paper Co., 165
Worthy Papers
    Item 178   165
Yeats, William Butler, 117
Young, Filson, 82
Ziegler, Lee Woodward, 182

Errata

A volume entitled *The Common Places of the moſt famous and renowmed Diuine Doctor Peter Martyr*, translated by Anthonie Marten and printed in London in 1583, contained upon completion only six discovered errors. The reader's indulgence is sought with such charm that we here repeat his plea, in the hope that it may distract your attention from our somewhat longer list.

Certaine Faults Escaped

There is no garden ſo well trimmed, but hath ſome weeds; no ſiluer ſo well tried, but hath ſome droſſe; no wine ſo well fined, but hath ſome leeze; no honie ſo well clarified, but hath ſome dregs; finallie, no humane action, but hath ſome defect: meruell not then (good Readers) that in ſo huge a volume, conſiſting of ſo manie leaues, lines, and letters, oftentimes varied both in forme and matter, a fault or two doo eſcape; were the Correctors care neuer ſo great, his diligence neuer ſo earneſt, his labour neuer ſo continual, his eies neuer ſo quicke, his judgement neuer ſo ſound, his memorie neuer ſo firme; breeflie, all his ſenſes neuer ſo actiue and liuelie. Such faults therefore as are paſſed, being but few in number, if it pleaſe you in reading fauourablie to amend, according as they be here corrected; your ſelues ſhall be profited, and I ſatisfied.

PAGE	LINE	CORRECTION
21	3	For *que* read *qua*
71	5, 17	For *E. M. Bird* read *E. B. Bird*
86	last	For *on* read *in*
88	6	For *on* read *in*
121	16	Omit *and Mr. Currier*
128	3	For *Mt. Vernon* read *New York*
136	last	Omit *done for Columbia*

Thefe are thought necefsarie to be noted; others (if anie be) I refer vnto your owne felues that fhall take paines to perufe the whole book aduifedlie.

Conclusion

In concluding this bibliography, a work which has been in preparation over eight years, I wish to acknowledge the assistance of numerous friends who have courteously loaned copies of Village Press publications for examination and have assisted in locating others. The woodcut frontispiece is reproduced by permission of the Typophiles. I am indebted to Will Ransom and to Frederic W. Goudy in particular; to the former for his unpublished diary, and the latter for his introductory biographical explanations, his illuminating notes on individual items, and his untiring assistance in bringing to light missing data.

ADDENDA TO
A Bibliography of The Village Press

Exhaustive bibliographies are seldom exhaustive. Father Time has a way of negativing the most thorough researches, revealing unsuspected titles in ways and places that are often something less than orthodox. The work of The Village Press is no exception, for the Pilgrimage to Deepdene, held July 23rd, 1938, in celebration of the thirty-fifth anniversary of the founding of the Press, occasioned the discovery of a further Village Press item.

The accommodation and comfort of the more than 200 guests, who had planned to attend, raised questions of convenience which determined Mr. Goudy to make certain alterations and installations on the ground floor of his house which had long been contemplated. These involved the demolition of an understairs closet, containing a box of books and papers placed there when the Goudys first moved to Marlboro and not since disturbed. It was in this forgotten collection that the fugitive item, which escaped record in *A Bibliography of The Village Press*, was found.

The author welcomes this opportunity to correct an error in Item 43, *The Lover's Hours*. The English publisher was Grant Richards, not John Lane as erroneously stated, and the sheets saved from the Parker Building fire were not bound, but simply folded into a Solander case.

It should likewise be mentioned that the authorities differ as to the further circumstances detailed in the last 5 lines of page 82. Mr. Goudy affirms and Mr. Kennerley denies the incident of the hotel, which was originally included on the authority of the former, who has since assured me of the accuracy of his statement. That this set of sheets was, somehow, preserved is all that really matters.

The Editor's fall from grace in the matter of the two following typographic errors, has been reported with ill-concealed delight by the discoverers:

PAGE	LINE	CORRECTION
2	22	For *omniverous* read *omnivorous*.
76	12	For *Ranson* read *Ransom*.

The following entry belongs on page 112:

84a. CATALOG OF AN EXHIBITION...

Twelve-page pamphlet, 6⅜ x 9¼ inches, self cover; sewed in red silk. *Catalog of An Exhibition Illustrating the Progress of the Art of Photography in America*, at the Montross Art Galleries, New York, Oct. 10-31. Foreword by Temple Scott and list of 148 photographs.

Set by hand in Tory and 14 point Village No. 2 by George W. Van Vechten, Jr., and illustrated with eight collotype reproductions, this book has been printed in an edition of 260 copies on Strathmore Permanent Book and completed in the month of April, 1938.

Printed at The Town House Press
Spring Valley, New York
MCMLXXXI